HUNTING DOGS

Hunting Dogs

Describes in a Practical Manner the Training, Handling, Treatment, Breeds, Etc., Best Adapted for Night Hunting as Well as Gun Dogs for Daylight Sport

---

BY
OLIVER HARTLEY

PUBLISHED BY
A. R. HARDING
COLUMBUS, OHIO
ISBN 0-936622-13-x

CONTENTS.

Part I — Hunting Dogs.

CHAPTER.		PAGE.
I.	Night Hunting	17
II.	The Night Hunting Dog — His Ancestry	33
III.	Training the Hunting Dog	39
IV.	Training the Coon Dog	49
V.	Training for Skunk, Opossum and Mink	59
VI.	Wolf and Coyote Hunting	65
VII.	Training for Squirrels and Rabbits	74
VIII.	Training the Deer Hound	80
IX.	Training — Specific Things to Teach	89
X.	Training — Random Suggestions from Many Sources	100

Part II — Breeding and Care of Dogs.

XI.	Selecting the Dog	107
XII.	Care and Breeding	116
XIII.	Breeding (Continued)	125
XIV.	Breeding (Continued)	133
XV.	Peculiarities of Dogs and Practical Hints	141
XVI.	Ailments of the Dog	146

Part III — Dog Lore.

XVII.	Still Trailers vs. Tonguers — Music	157
XVIII.	The Dog on the Trap Line	168
XIX.	Sledge Dogs of the North	178

Part IV—The Hunting Dog Family.

CHAPTER.		PAGE.
XX.	American Fox Hounds	193
XXI.	The Beagle, Dachshund and Basset Hounds	203
XXII.	Pointers and Setters. Spaniels	210
XXIII.	Terriers — Airedales	216
XXIV.	Scotch Collies. House and Watch Dogs	221
XXV.	A Farmer Hunter — His Views	228
XXVI.	Table of Technical Terms	242

LIST OF ILLUSTRATIONS

	PAGE
The Fruits of Night Hunting	16
The Court Jester of the Nocturnal Tribe	18
A Pure and a Cross-bred Coon Dog	20
Veteran Coon Detectives	28
Descendants from Jamestown Imported Hounds	32
Lovers of Good Dogs	38
A Fox Hound Graduate from the Training School	43
Typical Coon Hounds	48
Capable Cooners	55
A Good Catch in which the Dog Figured Prominently	58
Opossums are Easily Caught with the Aid of a Dog	61
Lion Dogs	64
Coyotes Caught with a Dog's Help	67
Termination of a Successful Chase	71
Good Dogs make Good Luck	73
Deer Caught with the Aid of a Dog	79
The Deer Seeks Refuge in Deep Water	81
Well Trained Hounds	85
Good Friends Get Along Best	90
Co-operation Between the Man and His Dogs Brings Results	99
Some Ideals	106
Embryo Trailers	115
A Versatile Breeder	124

LIST OF ILLUSTRATIONS.

	PAGE
Two Good Dogs with a Nice Catch	129
Fox Hounds	131
A Nice Pack of Hunting Dogs	132
Two Good Dogs and 14 Coon they Helped Dispatch	156
"He Was Here a Moment Ago"	164
"Here He Is"	166
A Group of Typical Sledge Dogs	177
Sledge Dog—Photo from Life	184
Rough and Ready Sledge Dog	187
A Worthy Fox Hound Aided with this Catch	192
Good Specimens	196
Blood Hound	199
"As Pretty as a Picture" (Beagles)	202
True Dachshund Specimens	205
A Pure Pointer	209
Royal Sports—Pointers in Action	211
Setter	213
The Fox Terrier—Useful in Many Ways	217
Airedale	218
Collie	222
Shepherd Puppies	226
Outline Figure Diagram	242

INTRODUCTION.

AS if hunting for profit, night hunting for either pleasure or gain and professional hunting generally had no importance, writers of books have contented themselves with dwelling on the study and presentation of matters relating solely to the men who hunt for sport only. Even then the Fox Chase and Bird Hunting has been the burden of the greater percent of such books.

It remained for the A. R. Harding Publishing Co. (publishers of Fur-Fish-Game—Harding's magazine and a number of helpful and practical books on hunting topics), to appreciate the demand for books and reading matter adapted especially to the tens of thousands of hunters who make, or partially make, their livelihood from hunting and trapping, as well as a million casual hunters and farmers of the United States and Canada.

The keynote of success was struck in this direction by obtaining articles and letters from these very men themselves, written and printed in their own language, depending for favor on their explicitness and practical value, borne of actual experience, rather than flowing language, high sounding conventionalities and impressive technicalities so dear to the hearts of the Bench Show enthusiasts.

The title of this book quotes its object. To tell something of night hunting, and especially to suggest how the ever necessary dog can best be selected, trained, maintained and utilized, is the consideration of first importance. To round out the subject all forms of hunting will receive some notice, and the various breeds of dogs will be so far dealt with, that their value and usefulness in their given fields may be determined. Best of all, the contents of this volume are based on the opinions and declarations of men who have had years of experience in the matters on which they presume to write. The Compiler does not assume authorship, the matter herein being very largely from articles which have appeared in Fur-Fish-Game magazine and elsewhere. Credit is hereby extended and our thanks offered to all writers whose efforts contribute to the sum total of this volume.

If this book contributes to the success in handling of dogs or opens new avenues of recreation, sport and profit for any of its readers, we shall consider its mission has been fulfilled.

OLIVER HARTLEY.

The Fruits of Night Hunting.

HUNTING DOGS.

CHAPTER I.

NIGHT HUNTING

NIGHT hunting is a favorite form of hunting sport the continent over. Prime factor of the joyous, though strenuous night quest is the 'coon, the court jester and wit of the nocturnal tribe of small fur bearers.

Owing to the scarcity of other game and general distribution of raccoon the country over, 'coon hunting is gaining in popular favor, winning over many of the wealthy, city-dwelling redbloods who formerly were content with more or less pleasant and successful sallies to the fields in the day-time.

Consequently there is an increased demand for properly bred and trained dogs to afford the maximum of success and pleasure in this pursuit. With the ownership of dogs go the care, maintenance and proper methods of handling these willing helpers. Surprising is the meagerness of the information available to the average

18 HUNTING DOGS.

hunter, though night hunting is an institution as old as the settlement of Jamestown.

The craft of developing dogs and using them to the best advantage in this connection, has been by precept and example handed down from generation to generation. Much has been lost in this way and not so much accomplished as might have been attained by aid of the printed and pictured methods of today. Most certainly more attention will hereafter be paid to night hunting, and more painstaking records made and

The Court Jester of the Nocturnal Tribe.

kept for the up-growing practical sportsmen, in which direction the present volume is a long and definite step.

Our task is to offer guidance and advice as to the dogs. Yet to do this clearly, the reader must know something of the nature and habits of the animals to be hunted and the effort involved.

A southern gentleman of experience and training has the following to say about 'coon hunting:

The 'coon is a wily little animal, and his habits are very interesting to note. He is a veritable trickster, compared with which the proverbial cunning fox must take a back seat. One of the 'coon's most common tricks employed to fool the hound is known among hunters as "tapping the tree," and which he accomplishes in this way: When he hears the hound's first note baying on trail, he climbs up a large tree, runs to the furthest extremity of one of the largest branches and doubling himself up into a ball, leaps as far as possible out from the tree. This he repeats several times on different trees, then makes a long run, only to go thru the same performances in another place. Onward comes the hound, till he reaches the first tree the 'coon went up, and if it is a young and inexperienced hound, he will give the "tree bark" until the

A Pure and A Cross Bred Coon Dog.

NIGHT HUNTING. 21

hunters reach the tree, fell it, and find the game not there.

All this time Mr. 'Coon is quietly fishing and laughing in his sleeve, perhaps a mile away. But not so with the wise old 'coon hound. The old, experienced 'cooner, with seemingly human intelligence, no sooner reaches the tree Mr. 'Coon has "tapped" than he begins circling around the tree, never opening his mouth — circling wider and wider until he strikes the trail again. This he repeats every time the 'coon takes a tree, until finally, when he has to take a tree to keep from being caught on the ground, the hound circles as before and, finding no trail leading away, he goes back to the tree, and with a triumphant cry proclaims the fact that he is victorious. He is not the least bit doubtful. He knows the coon went up the tree and he knows he has never come down so he reasons (?) that the coon is there, and with every breath he calls his master to come and bag his game. When the tree is felled the fun begins. The 'coon is game to death. He dies fighting — and such a magnificent fight it is! The uninformed might suppose there would not be much of a fight between a 50-pound 'coon hound and a 20-pound 'coon. Well, there is not, if the 'coon hound is experienced and knows his business. Of course, the 'coon will put up a masterly fight, and some time is required to put him out of business; but the old 'coon dog will finally kill any 'coon. But if the fight is between a young or inexperienced dog and a full grown 'coon the chances are that you will suffer the mortification of seeing your dog tuck his tail between his legs and make for home at a very rapid and unbecoming rate of speed.

To prove this, get a good 'coon hound and let him tree a 'coon; have along your Bull-dogs, Bull Terriers, Pointers, Setters, Collies, or any other breed you believe can kill a 'coon; tie your 'coon hound, cut the tree, and let your fighters on to the 'coon, one at a time or in a bunch, and see them clay him. You will see the old 'coon slap the faces off your dogs, and the shortest route home will be all too long for them.

Killing a 'coon appears to be an art with a dog, and, of course, much more easily acquired by a natural born 'coon hound than by a dog of any other breed. A year-old hound of good breeding and from good 'coon hound parents, can kill a 'coon with less ado about it than half a dozen of any other breed. It is in swimming that the 'coon is most difficult to handle. I have known several hounds to be drowned by 'coons in deep water. The dog goes for the 'coon, and the 'coon gets on top of the dog's head. Down they both go, and, of course, the dog and 'coon both let go their hold on each other. Again the dog grabs the 'coon, and under the water they both go. This is repeated, until the dog becomes exhausted, his lungs fill with water, and old Mr. 'Coon seems to understand the situation exactly and seats himself firmly on top of the dog's head, holding him under the water, till outside assistance is all that will save him from a watery grave.

As there is but little chance — practically none — to kill a 'coon while he is swimming, the wise old 'cooner, on to his job, will seize the 'coon, strike a bee line to the bank, and kill him on terra firma.

I once saw a big old boar 'coon completely outdo and nearly drown a half dozen young hounds in Hatchie River, when an old crippled hound, with not a tooth in his head, arrived on the scene, plunged into the river and brought Mr. 'Coon to the bank, where the young hounds soon killed him.

Another of the tricks Mr. 'Coon uses to advantage when closely followed by the hounds, is to follow the meanderings of a stream until he comes to a log reaching across to the other bank; then he runs to the middle of the log and leaps as far as he can out into the water, usually swimming down stream, as if he is not making for a den or a tree in some other direction. This ruse invariably delays even the best of 'coon hounds, as, being at about full speed, they will run on across the log, and if the dogs know their job they will circle out until they again find the trail; but during this momentary bother, the 'coon is not waiting to see what they are going to do about it. He keeps moving and I want to say that a 'coon is a much swifter traveler than many persons suppose. He delays no time, but keeps everlastingly at it, and it takes a speedy hound to force him up a tree.

The 'coon may be defined as being a dwarf bear. They have many points in common. The 'coon can lie up in his den for weeks at a time during severely cold weather, without food or water. The only difference between the foot prints of the coon and those of the bear is the size. In shape and appearance they are exactly alike. The flesh, when cooked, tastes similar, and not one in a thousand could tell any difference between cooked 'coon and cooked bear, if served in same size pieces.

By nature the 'coon is a very selfish individual. He deserts Mrs. 'Coon when his children are a day old and lets her provide for them as best she can. The young 'coons grow rapidly, and at the tender age of from six to eight weeks old they begin to accompany their faithful mother in search of food. Fishes, birds, rabbits, nuts, acorns, berries and green corn are the principal dishes on the 'coon family's bill of fare.

At first the little 'coons stay close to their mother's heels, but they grow more venturesome as they grow older, and soon begin to make little journeys on their own account. This often proves their undoing when dogs are about. Any sort of an old dog can tree or catch on the ground a baby 'coon, but this is an advantage no true sportsman will knowingly take.

That a mother 'coon will even brave death herself to save her babies is evident to one who has studied the habits of the 'coon. When closely pursued by the hounds and she and her young are all compelled to go up the same tree, as soon as the hounds begin to bark fiercely and the hunters arrive and begin to chop on the tree or to try to shine their eyes, old mother 'coon picks an opening and jumps out of the tree and is usually caught, or run up another tree close by and then caught. But she has again saved her young, as in all likelihood the hunters will not go back to the tree where the little coons are serenely sitting on the leafy boughs, or never think of there being any more coons there.

There are many reasons why the 'coon hunt is fast becoming one of the most popular of the manly sports. The 'coon is found in many sections of the United States. Other game is becoming very scarce. The wealthy business man, the man of affairs who is tied to his desk six days out of the week, can own a 'coon hound and in the stilly hours of the night, after the day's turmoil of business, can enjoy a few hours of the most strenuous sport now left to us and witness a battle royal between his faithful hound and the monarch of the forest, the wily 'coon. Nothing that I can contemplate is more exhilarating or more soothing to the nerves than the excitement of the 'coon hunt. From the first long drawn note when the trail is struck until the hound's victorious cry at the tree, it is one round of excitement and anticipation. What or whose hound is leading? What direction will Mr. 'Coon take? What dog will be first to tree? And then the fight! It is simply great! And then showing the hide to the boys who didn't go, and telling them about it for days to come.

The 'coon hunt calls for manhood. Tender weaklings cannot endure the exertions necessary to enjoy this sport. It is too strenuous for the lazy man or the effeminate man to enjoy. They shudder at the thoughts of donning a pair of heavy hip boots and tramping thru swamps and slashes, crossing creeks and barbed wire fences, thru briars and thickets, maybe for several miles, and the probability of getting lost and

NIGHT HUNTING. 27

having to stay all night. But to the man with nerve and backbone this is one of the enjoyable features. It affords great fun to get a tenderfoot to go out for the first time and initiate him into the "'coon hunters' club." The tenderfoot will use every cuss word ever invented and will coin new ones when the supply of old ones becomes worn out and ineffective. He will cuss the briars, cuss the ditches, cuss the creek, cuss the fences, cuss the swamps, cuss the slashes, cuss the man who persuaded him to go, and finally cuss himself for going. But when the excitement of the chase is on and when the fight commences he becomes reconciled; and if good luck is had he is very likely to be the next man to propose another "'coon hunt."

A half dozen hunts will make an enthusiastic 'coon hunter of any able bodied man — and I might suggest that a half a thousand 'coon hunts will make an able bodied man out of any man It will throw off the waste matter and dead tissues of the body, cause deep breathing, arouse torpid and sluggish livers, promote digestion, and is a general panacea for all human ailments of both mind and body."

(The foregoing contains much of value but is overdrawn even tho from the pen of a "Southern Gentleman" who should be well versed in 'coon hunting. Now and then a 'coon

28 HUNTING DOGS.

Veteran Coon Detectives.

will go up a tree and come down or even run out on a limb and jump off or may leap from a log across a stream into the water. Such instances, however, are rarely done to fool the dog. Generally when such happens, the 'coon has been feeding, going up and down trees, etc. When a 'coon does go up a tree, jump to another and similar tricks to fool a dog, that animal has been trailed before and is apt to be an "old timer.")

Added to this is the promise of other game, if the hunter is desirous of combining sport and profit. The skunk and opossum are common to many sections of this country. They are less resourceful and gritty than the 'coon, and their taking is simply a matter of choice and method, rather than concern for opportunities. A dog trained to hunt 'coon will have no trouble attending to opossum and skunk, if his owner desires it. Very frequently the trainer does not desire that his dog pay attention to anything save 'coon.

Still another profitable animal taken by night hunters is the mink. There is not so much sport in this branch, however, as the dogs simply trail or locate them in their dens, and are captured by digging or frightening them out, when they are dispatched by the dogs.

A good mink dog will often locate a mink in

the den during the day. If the den has more than one entrance, is not very deep in the ground, the animal will often run out by stamping or striking a few licks with a mattock. The mink generally comes out at the entrance nearest the water (quite often under water) when it can be shot, if you are quick enough, or if the dog is an active one, caught.

When hunting at night along streams, or places frequented by both mink and 'coon, it is sometimes difficult to tell, at first, which your dog is after. These two animals travel about the same along streams. Some dogs will not run mink unless especially trained while others take naturally to mink hunting. Unless a dog is not afraid of water, he will never make a good mink dog (or 'coon dog either for that matter), as mink go into a great many dens both on the bank and in the water.

Where the hunting is done in woods, considerable distance from streams or ponds and mink seldom travel, your dog may "pass them by" but if you should catch one in a trap and let him kill it, the chances are that you will have a mink dog.

Again by hunting certain stretches of creek where mink frequent, your dog will soon learn that you wish him to hunt these animals. A mink holed is far from caught, especially after

NIGHT HUNTING. 31

night. If holed in the creek bank, the chances are that the animal will dart out into the water and escape to another den.

The most successful mink hunting is done during the day by having your dog along and following the banks of creeks, lakes, ponds, etc. The dog locates the game and the animal is gotten out by methods already described.

Descendants from Jamestown Imported Hounds.

CHAPTER II.

THE NIGHT HUNTING DOG — HIS ANCESTRY.

DOGS of almost any breed, from the nondescript mongrel to the bred and developed hound may be taught to hunt in the woods at night. However, their success is, in a general way, in proportion to their adaptability for the work and the plentifulness of game. For instance, take a country raised dog of hound parentage, and he is as apt to make as good a night dog as a pedigreed, handsome hound which has grown up in the city, without opportunity to verify by experience his instinctive notion of things. Everything else being equal, the well bred hound should prove by far the better raw material for a good night hunter.

The ideal coon dogs of most experienced night hunters are the half bred fox hounds. Thus is enlisted the training of centuries to match the wits of the 'coon which was born wily, and develops strategem from experience and necessity, affording as exciting and pretty a contest (dog vs. coon) as sport provides.

The more one knows of the hound he follows, the greater will be his enjoyment and success.

He will avoid blaming the dog with his own mistakes, and wisely refrain from trying to exact from the dog what by physique and breeding he was not intended by nature to do.

How the modern fox hound descended from the blood hound and the coon hound from the fox hound is an interesting study of more or less importance in striking an estimate of the coon dog's prowess and abilities. It is not such a far cry from the exciting man hunt of other days to the coon hunt of the present.

What we call the native American foxhounds are descended from dogs brought over from England, Ireland and France. The settlers at Jamestown imported the hounds that spread out over the southern frontier, originating the superb packs to be found throughout the South to-day.

The imported dog has never proven a good performer in the chase, owing to very widely different conditions encountered. His value has been in cross breeding to give bone and substance to native breeds.

Says one authority: By selection and a different character of work, we have produced a lighter, faster hound than the ancestral type. Our hounds are required to go and search for a fox. That quality has become instinctive in them and it is an extremely necessary natural quality.

What we have really done in this country with the fox-hound is, we have created a new type. Our native hounds which are without any near English or Irish hound crosses are not only faster than their ancestors, but they get about in rough country, quicker and with greater ease. The American bred dog, long accustomed to hunting, may be readily developed to night hunting.

There are some strains of native hounds that train easier than others. Hounds that have come down through an ancestry which have long been in large packs have certain fixed notions or instincts about hunting that are more difficult to change than are hounds which have grown up singly or in couples.

Whatever manner of hound the trainer may undertake to develop it is well for him to consider the dog's ancestry and the way in which they have been hunted. He will find if his hound is well bred that the ancestral influence will tend to assert itself. Knowing what is in his hound, the trainer will know better how to handle him to bring him up to the highest possible degree of efficiency.

There were many different breeds of the hound family existing in England, when the fox hound, the great grandfather of the typical night hunter under consideration, began to assume a fixed type and receive recognition.

"A popular error" writes another authority, 'into which many writers have fallen is to associate the fox hound with any one or two breeds of hounds for his common ancestry, for the fact is that both the English and American fox hound is a composite animal, descended from many different varieties of hounds which have existed in the past."

There are a number of breeds of hounds in France to-day that cannot be intelligently traced to any peculiar origin and there have been a greater variety of hounds in the past, which have found the way into the kingdom by different roads.

It will never be known exactly what hunting qualities the hounds of our crude forefathers possessed or with what melody of tongue, accuracy of scent, or fleetness of foot they pursued game, which consisted, with now and then an exception, of the stag, wild boar and wolf, until the gradual advance of civilization drove the larger animals from denuded forest and left the cunning fox as the logical object of especial attention to huntsmen, who have spared neither time nor expense to accomplish his death legitimately for nearly two centuries.

Summing up we are impressed with the fact that the perfect fox or coon hound is a superb physical being of most versatile and capable properties, subject to our beck and call, if we learn the language of the chase, before we attempt to tell him what is wanted.

Let us go to the next important topic, Training the Night Hunter, with due respect and humility. Success in training a fine performer is a credit to a man; failure is a discredit. Heed well the advice of experienced men, and profit by their mistakes.

38   HUNTING DOGS.

Lovers of Good Dogs.

CHAPTER III.

TRAINING THE HUNTING DOG.

IN training hounds, one should remember that they will always have a hobby for the first game they learn to hunt; therefore, we should be careful to start them first at the right kind as for instance: If you desire to have an all around hound that will hunt coon, fox and rabbit and to hunt each game well, and in order to succeed you must break him in on coon first, then when he knows the "A, B, C," of Mr. Coon, you can break him on foxes and then on rabbits in the day time and when you will hunt coon he will pay no attention to the fox or rabbit even if he would see one in front of him, providing there are coons in that bush.

If you desire to have a true deer hound, train him first on deer, then on foxes, but you must in all cases train them well on one kind before you start on another; therefore, a hound thus trained will always hunt deer in preference to fox. The same would exist if the dog was first trained on the fox.

Some people claim that it takes from three to five years to train a hound right. Well, this is not always the case. Young hounds twelve to fifteen months old are often taken from the city into the bush and in three days would hunt deer as well as other dogs of five and six years' training. The reason for this is that these dogs take as naturally to hunting as ducks do to water. These dogs are born with the hunting instinct in them and being very intelligent, will start at once to beat a bush as well as an old timer, as soon as they have seen the game once they will remember it all their life and you can train them to hunt any kind whether it is a bear, deer, fox, etc.

Of a necessity in treating on the general subject of training hunting dogs, some suggestions are applicable to all kinds, while others have individual bearing. Under the subject of this chapter will be given subdivisions relating to specific training for specific hunting in so far as required.

There are some fundamental lessons that all hunting dogs should be taught to do and some things which he is not to do.

Let him begin to follow you when he is three or four months old; take him through herds of sheep and cattle, and if he starts after them, scold him; if he continues chasing them, whip him. I do not believe in whipping where it can be avoided, but if compelled to, do not take a club or a No. 10 boot, but a switch; and I never correct a dog by pulling his ears for fear of hurting his hearing, as a dog that is hard of hearing is not an A No. 1 dog. Never set your dog on stock of any kind nor allow him to run after other dogs or house-cats.

By the time he is four months old, he will

"The Fox Hound is a Composite Animal."

likely begin to run rabbits, but some do not commence until older. Let him run them as it will teach him to trail and harden his muscles, and, should you have more than one, it will teach them to depend on each other, and they will soon learn to go to other dogs when they start a trail or pick up a loss. If you have a fox or coon hide to drag or a pet to lead, it will not do any harm, though I do not think it of much value as they soon learn to associate your tracks with those of the fox or coon, and I greatly prefer letting them run rabbits as a mode of training them.

By the time they are eight months old, take them out with a slow dog that runs and barks a great deal, both trailing and running, and as soon as the fox is running, let your pup go, but do not let him go until the old dog has passed with the fox. Should you let him go meeting the old dog he may take the back track, but if you wait until the old dog has passed your pup, he will come in behind, and, if he is bred right, will go in and stay as long as he can find a trail to follow.

If he should come out after a short run, keep him until the fox is tired; then let him go again, and if he still continues to come out after a few times, don't fool with him, but try him for something else. If your pup has been in good trim, and has come out three times on fair trials, there is very little chance of making a fox dog out of him.

I have had pups of this kind which I kept until they were two years old; have bought pet foxes, and let them catch and kill them, but never yet made a runner out of a dog that it was not born in.

TRAINING THE HUNTING DOG. 43

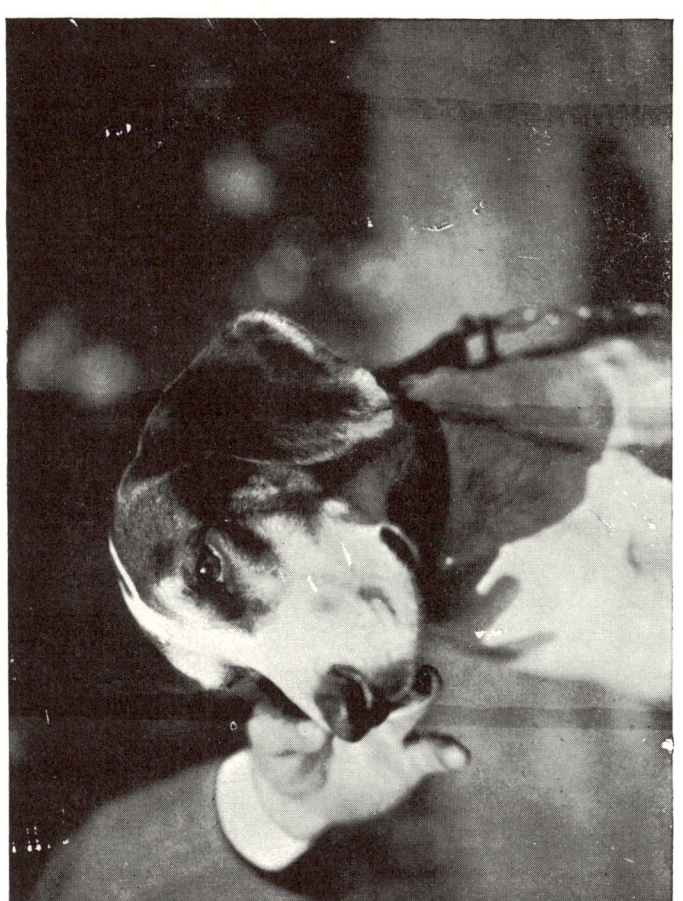

A Fox Hound Graduate from the Training School

Should your pup go in and stay, don't run him too often unless he is near a year old. Never take him out unless he is well fed, and in good shape to run. After a race or two let him go as soon as the trail is struck, and after a few races, catch the old dog, after the fox is going, and see what the pup will do alone. Then take them out on a good day, let the old dog pick up the trail, and after the pups have started, catch the old dog and let the pups go alone, and if they trail, start and run that fox to a finish, that is all the pedigree they will ever need.

When you turn your dog loose, don't run and yell and get him so excited that he doesn't know what to do, just unbuckle his collar and let him go. If he does not understand going into a race, it will not help matters to excite him, just walk to where the fox has passed and he will likely take the trail, and will know better what to do the next time.

When your dogs are running and happen to lose the trail near you, do not run and call, trying to help them get started, for if let alone they are far more apt to pick it up and go on in good shape; by getting them excited and running wild the chase would likely end right there.

My rule is this: Whenever I pull a dog's collar, he must look out for No. 1 without my going to show him.

TRAINING THE HUNTING DOG. 45

Should you not have an old dog to help train your pup, you can train him alone, but it is more trouble.

If you have snow, lead your dog until you find a fox trail, then follow it, still leading your dog; if there happens to be considerable scent in the trail, he may want to follow it, if so turn him loose, but follow him up and help him to start his fox. If there is no scent in the trail, lead your dog until you start the fox, then let him go and let him work for himself.

Should you have neither snow nor trained dog, you will have more trouble, but I have made No. 1 dogs without either.

If you know where foxes stay, go there, turn your dog loose, and he will start to running rabbits; this will scare the fox up and your dog will likely cross its track; if he is a born fox dog, he will leave the rabbit for the fox every time. You may have to make several trips, but after you get one race, your dog will be looking for a fox chase, and will soon take a cold fox trail in preference to a rabbit.

After you have trained your dog to running foxes or coon, you will wish to break him of running rabbits; this is generally an easy matter, for a genuine dog prefers the fox or coon and some will quit it of their own accord. If not, try scolding him when he starts a rabbit. If that fails, whip him, but where foxes are plentiful, you will seldom have to do this.

My pups are accustomed to the crack of a 22 rifle, as I shoot near them while young, so never have any gun-shy dogs.

There is just as much in feeding a running dog, as a running horse. Some say a light feed just before starting and I have heard some say, don't feed at all. Now for a grey fox, it does not make so much difference, as the chase will only last an hour or two, and sometimes not ten minutes, but where it comes to an old red fox, — one that you start Saturday night and return just in time to accompany your wife to church next morning, it is quite different.

A dog to do his best should be used to running. He should have a few days' rest, and if his feet are sore, grease once each day with salty grease. At least three days before the race, drop all sloppy food and give rye or corn-bread with scraps from the butcher shop mixed in before baking. Feed liberally twice each day and if your race promises to be a hard one, feed extra before starting, some food that will give the greatest amount of strength, with the least possible bulk. Then arrange to give your dog a good heavy feed as soon as he returns home, and he will be ready for the next race sooner than if compelled to go to rest hungry.

Before closing, I will say something more with regard to breeding: — We often see where someone has pure bred Walker, Williams, Redbone or Buckfield Blues. Now to my understanding, these are strains of dogs, bred by southern fox hunters, 50 or 75 years ago, and to keep them pure, there must have been a lot of inbreeding, a thing I do not approve of. Now why would it not have been better for Mr. Walker to have selected one of his very best bitches and bred her to one of Mr. Williams' best dogs, then called the pups the "American Fox Hounds"—as grand a dog as ever put his nose to a trail?

48 HUNTING DOGS.

Typical Coon Hounds.

CHAPTER IV.

TRAINING THE COON DOG.

IN training, we have been told to drag a 'coon hide, lead a pet 'coon, etc., but your pup soon learns to associate your tracks with the trail of the drag, and when you carry the 'coon hide he simply follows your track to where you start the drag again. Should you have a 'coon so tame that it will follow you, start out and tramp through the woods, along streams and just such places as 'coons frequent. Your 'coon will run logs, go up on the side of trees, in and out of the water, in fact will do just about as a wild 'coon would. After you have been gone for some time, have someone turn your pup on the trail and if he runs it, keep him a little later each time, and you will soon have a trailer out of him anyway. Should you have neither 'coon nor old dog, you can train your pup without.

In nearly all places where there are 'coons, squirrels and woodchucks (groundhogs) may be found also. Teach your dog to lead and when he is about eight months old, attach a light cord to his collar; then some good morning for squirrels, take him to the woods. Keep him until he gets sight of a squirrel, then drop the cord and let him go; he will likely see it run up a tree, and perhaps he will bark, but if not, do not urge him, but give him plenty of time; then take him to find another and if he does not get to barking, get one in small timber, where you can make it jump from tree to tree; if he does not bark then, he will never be much of a 'coon dog.

If he barks after he has learned to tree squirrels, take him to a woodchuck country. He will soon get to working after woodchucks and while they won't all tree, some of them will, Should he get one in a hole, hollow log or tree, get it for him if possible and let him kill it, and see that he doesn't get hurt much. If he trees one, shoot it out for him, and after he has gotten a few, and trees another, go to where you can see him, but do not let him see you, and watch until he starts to leave; then go to him and by so doing, he will learn to stay and wait for you.

After you have a good dog for woodchucks, you may rest assured that he will tree a 'coon if he finds a trail. If it happens to be summer time, take him where 'coons abide and turn him loose. He will likely run rabbits, but when he strikes a 'coon trail, he will take it. As soon as you know he is after a 'coon, keep after him as near as possible, but let him have his own way. If he trees it and barks, get to him as soon as you can, but do not urge him, for he will get to lying as soon as you want him to without any help from you.

After he has barked awhile, encircle the tree with him; then if the 'coon has been up and gone on again, he will strike his trail, and, after a few times, he will learn to circle before barking. If the 'coon is up and it is summer time or early fall, when 'coon hides are not prime, take your dog back from the tree, keep still, and unless it is a den tree, you won't have long to wait, for another 'coon chase, and by keeping your dog longer each time, you will soon have a cold trailer out of him.

This may seem considerable work for some, but it takes work and time to make even a fair 'coon dog. Should you have a good dog to train with, it saves lots of work, but even then it is a good plan to work early in the season, and tree your 'coon several times in one night, as you do not have far to go after the first tree.

In breeding 'coon dogs, the same rule applies as in fox dogs — if your dog is bred from a line of 'cooners, he will take to it naturally. Some one will say, I will take a house cat to teach my dog to tree. Well I have done that myself, but after cutting several good trees, only to get a house cat, I learned better. It is just as easy to break a dog from running cats, as rabbits, and more so. I do not consider a dog that will run and tree every house cat he strikes the trail of, a No. 1 'coon dog, no matter what his other good qualities may be.

Years ago, when timber was more plentiful than now, I always trained my dog to take care of himself, when a tree was cut for 'coons, and I never had a dog get hurt, nor had many 'coons to get very far from the tree.

They are easily taught by cutting small trees in the day time and making them keep back until the tree is down; but now, timber is getting rather scarce and valuable to cut for 'coons.

When a dog is trained for 'coon so that he is first class, he is valuable in dollars and cents as well as satisfaction. One of our good friends sets the value in this way, and we agree with him, except that where one is training a dog for his own use, love of the pursuit and woods repays him in a measure for his trouble:

"A man ought not to expect to get a first class 'coon dog for five or ten dollars. In fact, one can't be trained for that price, not saying anything about his feed. In the first place stop and consider how many nights one has to be

TRAINING THE COON DOG. 53

taken out to get him to understand running them, and to learn their tricks and to tree and stay treed. They may do this in a reasonably short time with another older, well trained dog to show them how to find the tree and keep them out there, but then take him out by himself and when Mr. 'Coon goes in the creek or around an old pond or bog your young dog lacks experience and a year's work or more.

Then there is the rabbit which he must be broken not to run, and a dog can always find their tracks before he can a 'coon. Now here is where the right kind of judgment must be used, as all dogs cannot be handled alike, and one may spoil a pup in trying to break him from rabbits. So taking everything into consideration, it is worth far more to train a dog for a first class 'coon dog than most people consider, — what it requires to train a dog, and what he should be worth when properly broken.

Of course, it is not so much work to train a dog to run fox, as there is generally a lot of fox dogs one can turn in with, and that way get a young dog started and he will take to running them naturally."

I think a good dog, either a fox hound, or one that has never run foxes, makes the best dog, altho curs or 'coon dogs are not to be kicked out, that is if they are good, true hunters. I wouldn't advise trying to train a hound with a cur unless he is an old 'coon dog. Try and get your dog on a 'coon right in the start, and do not let him fight too much the first time, unless he is an extra fighter. Do not let your dog stay out hunting when the other dogs have treed a 'coon; make him come in and bark up the tree. Always climb the tree for your dog and get what he has, no matter if it takes until daylight.

When I own young dogs, I always train them myself. I never permit a stranger to handle them. It is all right for strangers to handle the old dogs once they are trained but the hunter who wishes to have good dogs should train them himself or have a man who thoroughly understands the proper way to use young dogs. It is a very easy matter to spoil a dog when you do not know exactly how to proceed.

On the question of the proper age at which to begin training a hound, a successful Minnesota trainer takes issue with those who advise taking the pup to field at eight or ten months of age. He writes in part: "I disagree with those who advise the early initiation of the pup. Any kind of fairly well bred pup will run, not only at 10 months, but at 5, 6 or 7 months, but the point to consider is, will a dog

Capable Cooners.

put at hard work at such age, become a hardy one? Will he develop himself as well as if he had been given a chance to grow some bones? I say no; put a colt at hard work at 2 or 3 years old, will he ever be the horse which he would have been, if he had only been broken at 4 or 5 years old? Every horse breeder knows that if he wants a good roadster, he must give him a chance to grow, then he will not be afraid to cover 60 or more miles in a day with that horse; not only this but he will get many times the price for that horse as for his brother which was put to work two years earlier. I have bred horses and know of what I speak.

There are many reasons why a sportsman should not start to train his dog to hunt before he is full grown, that is at least not until he is 12 to 15 months old. Before that age, a pup may have the will but he has not the strength to cover the ground of an old dog. A man who has a valuable pup should wait until he is capable to stand hardships, and until he has also a good knowledge box. In allowing a pup of 6, 7, 8 or 10 months to hunt, he will learn more bad tricks than good ones, such as to remain in the bush longer than necessary, and soon become a long record dog. The risk is great that he will get lost, or if not, will return with swollen feet and legs if he ran at all, also be chilled and

TRAINING THE COON DOG.

be rewarded with a fine dose of distemper. This is often the cause why so many young dogs die with distemper or of some other lingering death, but if a man gives time to his dog to develop and get strong, the chance is, should he ever get distemper, it would be but a slight attack from which he will soon recover."

We take it, however, that our well informed friend does not mean to imply that a pup should not be taken afield and given a kindergarten course earlier than a year old. His contention is, no doubt, that the pup should not be permitted to over exert himself or to be thrown too much on his own resources.

A Good Catch in which the Dog Figured Prominently.

CHAPTER V.

TRAINING FOR SKUNK, OPOSSUM AND MINK.

ALL the foregoing has more or less application to the present topic. We are still dealing with the nocturnal wanderers. Occasionally any of the above may be discovered abroad in the full glare of day. Some hunters successfully locate them, by the aid of dogs, in their dens or burrows and capture them in the day-time. This is a cut and dried operation that requires none of the resourceful tactics of man and dog in the chase, and is, therefore, dismissed from the discussion.

Now, what are the dog's duties? The matter of still hunters vs. tonguers, being of such variance of opinion, it will be discussed in a subsequent and separate chapter.

Having impressed your dog with the fact that you want him to look out for skunk, possum and mink, as well as 'coon, the next point of importance is to insist on the dog staying with the quarry and barking until you arrive; also not to take hold until the word is given as the hide is apt to be all chewed up and full of holes if the dog is too long and too vigorous in the task. Many hunters pick up many of the skunk on the field, without even being touched by the dogs.

In this connection a contributor writes: "We walk right up to the skunks and pick them up by the tails; then hit them on the head with a club and kill them or put them in the bag and take them home alive, as the occasion may suit."

"Now, I won't tell that I can catch skunks without getting scented, but will say this, we have caught hundreds by the tail, and after lifting them clear off the ground, never have been scented by them. As I said before, I go for the business end of it, and am not afraid to get some scent on me as long as I don't get it in my eyes. If you get it in your eyes, it feels about as if you had horse-radish or hot water in them for the next ten minutes, which is not altogether pleasant."

The skunk is a foolish, unresourceful animal and were it not for its natural, unique means of defense, would be utterly at the mercy of dogs and hunters. Many dogs object to the scent and will trail and bring to bay a skunk only with reluctance. Only those who hunt for profit, care to take the skunk, and he must needs learn the finer points by experience.

The Scotch Terrier and Beagle should be

a good mink dog. This combination gives the requisite agility needed in coping with mink. Some even advise a strain of water Spaniel with the above breed for an ideal cross for mink as

Opossums are Easily Caught with the Aid of a Dog.

well as rabbit. However the steel trap is more generally relied upon to bag the sly mink as his capture with dog and gun is often very unproductive.

"Before taking him out you can teach the young dog when 8 or 10 months old, what to do by catching an animal that you wish to train your dog on and leading it around. If it is a 'coon or opossum, then put up a tree or on a fence. Loose your dog and let him trail until he finds it. Teach the dog to bark by hissing him on and clapping, whooping to him and such like.

If for skunk, kill one and drag it around, place it out of pup's reach, and teach him to bark when he comes upon his game. You can teach the habit of tongueing after night or silence on the trail as you prefer. Let your young dog shake and chew at the game you are training him to hunt for. After he has found it and he fails to bark by hissing him, tie a rope three feet long to it and keep throwing it toward him and pulling it quickly away to teach him to grab at it and hold on, and also bark. A live skunk generally gives a young dog such a lesson the first time that he is always afraid of one afterwards, unless he is an Irish terrier or bull dog or beagle crossed. These two breeds are good ones for any kind of night hunting.

Take a live animal, a 'coon or something, and lead it past your young dog's box where he is tied and let him see it and take notice how he will want it, but all you want is to teach him the scent and how to tongue when he comes up on

TRAINING FOR SKUNK, OPOSSUM, ETC.

the game. I believe what I have told will generally break any dog.

A good dog, well broken to hunt 'coon, skunk of opossum is worth scores of traps. Don't be afraid to switch a young dog some, to make him learn good from bad, like tongueing track and rabbit. Always pet him and be friendly after chastising him, and a good scolding with a couple of light smacks with open hand will take the place of a whipping. Don't use a stick unless necessary. Use judgment, the same as you would want some one to use you, and in a few nights' training your dog will be catching game. It is easy sailing after a few are caught, and your dog is your greatest friend you have. He will make you from $5.00 to $15.00 a night, where if you were trapping for the same game, you would be lucky if you got a dollar's worth of fur, and besides what is finer sport than a day's gunning, to hear your old dog up on yonder hill or in some woods talking to you to come his way?"

Lion Dogs.

CHAPTER VI.

WOLF AND COYOTE HUNTING.

IN training a dog to run wolves, it is unsafe to allow a young dog to go alone, as some wolves prefer fighting to running, and if a young dog is whipped back a few times, he will become afraid, or will be perhaps, spoiled altogether. Training a dog to hunt young wolves is a harder task, and unless your dog is born for it, you will fail to make anything like a first class dog out of him. Almost any good fox dog will hunt old wolves, but very few will hunt pups, and my experience has been that a bitch will hunt quicker than a dog. There are a great many dogs that will trail and hunt a wolf to a finish, but will pay no attention to the pups whatever; but if you succeed in finding one that is inclined to hunt them, remember that practice makes perfect.

Speaking of brush wolves: The kind of dog needed is a good ranger, extra good cold trailer and an everlasting stayer. Then if he will only run a short distance after starting the wolf and come back and hunt the pups, and then bark at them when found, you have a good, valuable dog. There are plenty of dogs that will hunt and trail wolves all right, but very few that will hunt the pups.

Sometimes when your dog trails in near the pups you will get a fight, and sometimes they will jump out and run for it. Sometimes if the pups are quite young you will find the mother in with them and for the first few days she will be found near them, but as they grow older she will be found farther away.

A Minnesota wolfer who averages 35 wolves a year pins his faith in the long eared variety of hounds, with features of strength, endurance, good tonguers and stayers.

From another source we are advised that the best dogs ever for coyotes, are part English blue and Russian stag. English blue are very fast and the stag are long winded and have the grit to make a good fight.

Another admired and capable dog is the one-half Scotch stag hound and one-half grey hound.

A Wisconsin hunter writes that the best breed to catch and kill coyotes are one-half shepherd and one-half hound. They are faster than a hound and trail just as well on a hot trail.

Another fast breed for coyotes is a one-fourth English bull, one-fourth blood hound and one-half fox hound.

WOLF AND COYOTE HUNTING.

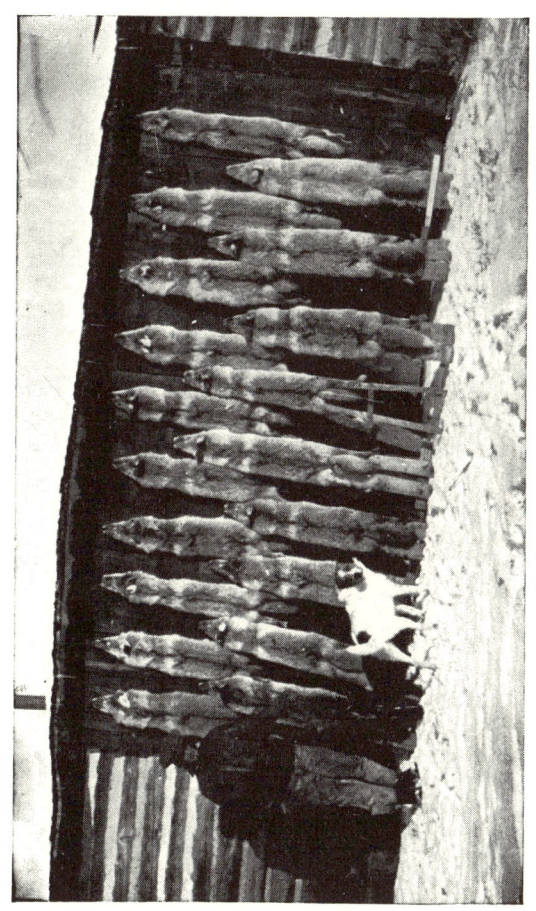

Coyotes Caught with a Dog's Help.

A Kansas hunter contributes some first hand discussion of wolf hunting as follows: I have been hunting wolves with dogs for eight or nine years and have caught my share. I only hunt in spring and late in fall, but any time is good when you can find them. But don't take your dogs out in summer, as it will be sure to be the time when you will find a hard race, and there is where you will hurt some of your best dogs. I use a pack of from three to five, but the more the better.

I have tried most all kinds of dogs and have found a cross with stag hound and English greyhound suits me the best. I don't have any use for a full blood English greyhound — they cannot stand the cold weather and are too easily hurt in a fight.

I want a dog that will weigh 75 pounds, with long legs and short back so he can gather himself up quickly. I don't think foxhounds are any good for wolves. I have seen thirty-five of them start after the same wolf, in good weather and four hours afterward there were only two, the smallest of the pack, still in the race. I have no doubt but that they could have taken the wolf several times in the race, but all they could do was to bark.

I will not say a full blood stag hound is not all right, in a level, unobstructed country, but in many parts of the country many large dogs would not be able to get thru the fences or over the rough ground with the ease that the smaller ones do.

I have never seen the big dog that could catch and kill a wolf by himself. I have killed them with two, but would rather have four or five.

I always hunt on a horse, and they should be the best of horses, well broken and not afraid of wire. I never carry a gun of any kind, but always have a hammer, and if I want to succor the dogs in the race, I will ride up to the dogs and kill the wolf for them.

THE IRISH WOLFHOUND.

The Irish wolfhound of history is no more, the breed having become extinct years ago. There has been a determined effort, however, to approximate him with a present day breed. The modern Irish wolfhound is a cross between the Scottish deerhound and the Great Dane. Other combinations have also been tried, with more or less good effect.

According to the idea of the American-Irish Wolfhound Club, the Irish wolfhound should be "not quite so heavy or massive as the Great Dane, but more so than the deerhound, which in general type he should resemble. Of great size and commanding appearance, very muscular, strongly though gracefully built; movements easy and active, head and neck carried high; the tail carried with an upward sweep, with a slight curve toward the extremity.

The minimum height and weight of dogs should be 31 inches and 120 pounds; bitches 28 inches and 90 pounds. Anything below this should be debarred from competition. Great size, including height and shoulder and proportionate length of body is the desideratum to be aimed at, and it is desired to firmly establish a race that shall average from 32 to 34 inches in dogs, showing the requisite power, activity, courage and symmetry."

"The coat should be rough and hard on body, legs and head; especially wiry and long over the eyes and under the jaws. The recognized colors are gray, brindle, red, black, pure white, fawn or any color that appears in the deerhound."

THE RUSSIAN WOLFHOUND.

The Russian wolfhound has a reputation for being a most capable wolf-catcher in his native country, but so far the pure bred hound of that family has not held his own with the

WOLF AND COYOTE HUNTING. 71

Termination of a Successful Chase.

American wolf. He has the speed and capacity for catching the wolf, but is unable to cope with him or detain him long enough for the hunter to arrive. Admirers of the dog say he lacks training and adaption and that he will with a generation or two of careful training and practice become the most available dog for the purpose.

Others get good results by crossing in some fiercer and stronger blood.

The Russian Wolfer has somewhat the clean cut appearance of the greyhound, though more stockily built, and has a long, silky coat of wavy or curly hair.

"In general appearance" says an authority, "he is an elegant, graceful aristocrat among dogs, possessing courage and combining great muscular power with extreme speed, weighing from 75 to 105 pounds."

Good Dogs Make Good Luck.

CHAPTER VII.

TRAINING — FOR SQUIRRELS AND RABBITS.

HERE is my way for training squirrel and coon hounds, which I think is best, writes a Texas Hunter. First, select good healthy pups, raise them up friendly and don't whip or cow them in any way until about ten or twelve months old, for if pups get cowed when young they will never get over it. When about ten months old, take them out hunting with one or two squirrel dogs and then when the old dogs tree in small trees or any place where you can make them jump out, jump the squirrel out and get your pups after them.

Then if the squirrel gets up another tree your pups will bark up the tree at him. Then when they bark well up the tree at the sqiurrel, pet, sick and yell to let the pups know that you are trying to help them catch the squirrel. Keep jumping the squirrel out until they catch him, and if they don't catch him and it gets away up a big tree where you can't jump him, then shoot him and they will wool him when he falls out.

Clean the squirrel and give the pups some of it to eat, and you won't be but a few times out

TRAINING FOR SQUIRRELS AND RABBITS. 75

hunting squirrels and jumping them out for the pups and trying to help them catch the squirrel until they will start out hunting and treeing squirrels as good as any old dog. If the dogs won't bark up the tree when you get through all of this and they see the squirrel run back up the tree, you might as well kill them or take them and run deer, for they will never make tree dogs.

The following directions for perfecting the rabbit dog, are from the pen of an experienced and successful Ohio hunter.

Get your pup some day while young, if possible, keep him by you, and when you see a sparrow or something alive, shoot it, pick it up and show him what you shot at; do this at home. Shoot all you please while he is young, so when you go hunting with him and shoot at game he won't be afraid and make a bee line for home.

Most dogs will soon take a liking to guns. Now to training a beagle dog to be a good one on rabbits, I warn you never to take another dog along, but for a common hound you may use your own way.

I have seen good beagle dogs spoiled by other dogs. Now, some frosty morning take your pup to where you most think there are rabbits; scare one out, and then if he is not near, give three good sharp whistles which you ought to keep as your signal for him to come. If you train your pup to a regular code of whistles, he will know what you want. So here is a good code, which if kept in rule, will become very handy. When you have scared up game let three sharp whistles be the calling; if you only want him to come to go another way, give three long ones. Motion your hand in what direction you want to go and he will soon learn to understand.

I have often let the dog decide the way to go. Now to go back to the old subject, when he comes you must be all excited and showing him that you are greatly in need of him. Then show him three of four places where the rabbit hopped; when he gets a start you go and stand where you most think he will come around, but again I warn you never to jump and run away while your pup is near enough to see or even hear you, for if you do, he will leave the track and follow you. Also, you will do a fine piece of work to shoot the first rabbit he brings around.

Now when you shoot the game, pick it up and wait until your dog comes, then show it to him, but never let him eat one, for if you only cripple one he will catch and eat it. Teach him in the start to hold game until you come to him. Now to get him to start to hunt another rabbit may be your trouble. He may want to stay with you and try to steal your rabbit. The best way to start him out is to start walking through the brush and stamping on brush piles, at the same time telling him to "hunt 'em up." Keep a piece away from him and he will soon start to hunt again. Now if he runs one into a den, what should you do? Dig 'im out and be a "Johnny-dig-'em-out" or let him go.

Better examine the first den, and if not over 2 or 3 feet deep and only a small hole, you may dig it out, if it is one of your dog's first hunts, but don't dig very big dens, for by the time you dig one out, you may get a shot at another. The way to get your pup away from a den is to look the situation over and then give up, telling him to give it up; we can't get it; he will soon come away.

There are other things to be careful of; first you should never hurry your dog; walk slow and when he gets used to hunting let him scare up the most of the game or he will get lazy and want you to be the dog. Never whip your dog for a mistake, or you may spoil him. Then when you come home you may give him the rabbit heads. Let him in the house, and when you eat your rabbit, give him all the bones. This will teach him why and for what you take your game home. One great thing is, if your dog scares up game and is following on the trail, don't change your standing place too often; judge the point where the game will come around and stay there until it does come.

Some fellows will run, jump and halloo

after his dog while running a rabbit; there is where you spoil him, for you must be cool in mind. Then when your dog is running a rabbit and night is coming on, don't go home until your dog comes to you, or right there is where your dog will be discouraged. So when the day's hunt is over you can go home with your dog by your side.

While you are showing him what good he did for you, if he is wet and cold call him near the stove and dry him. For if a dog must lay outside all wet, he will soon become stiff in his limbs, and rheumatism will be seen at an early age. Always after the day's hunt, give him all he wants to eat. Don't have him too fat in hunting season, because he will tire out too easily.

TRAINING FOR SQUIRRELS AND RABBIT. 79

Deer Caught with the Aid of a Dog.

CHAPTER VIII.

TRAINING THE DEER HOUND.

ON all things there is a main point, also certain rules which should never be forgotten in training hounds, especially the age and the way to train them. My experience has taught me that it is a big mistake to allow a young deer hound to go in the woods before he is 12 to 15 months old," says a Canadian hunter.

At a year old a hound should know how to lead well, that is not to pull on the chain for all he is worth ahead of his master but to follow behind him through every place he passes, if between, under or over logs as well as fences, to follow exactly the same trail as his master. A dog or a pair coupled together, so trained, can be easily led in any bush without any bother whatever. It is not at all necessary that a dog should lead in front of his master to find a trail. A dog with a keen nose can pick a trail from the air several yards before reaching it. He will then pull you in the direction of the same and if the scent is fresh, he will be anxious to follow it, then if the hunter is a man who understands his business, he will examine the track by following it 100 yards or so and if suitable and going (if it is a deer) in the right direction and if the wind is also right, will then allow his hound to go.

A dog which knows his business will not open the minute he gets the scent but will cover the ground fast and save his steam until he has jumped the deer or fox, then open his value and

The Deer Seeks Refuge in Deep Water.

if he is a flyer he will water more deer in five hours than another which gives tongue as soon as he takes the scent in five days for the reason that a dog which opens the very instant he finds a trail will have to cover 20 times more ground to bring his deer to water, than the one which does not.

A hound should not be gun or water shy but should be shy of strangers, traps and of poisoned baits. He should know how to swim across a river or lake and where to land. He should have but one master and obey him to the word and this without the use of the whip. He should know how to ride in a canoe. All this can be taught to him in about 3 months and he should know all these things before he is broken to hunt.

The next thing is to accustom your dog to the gun. This is easily done. All you have to do is to take your gun and dog into a field and once there to tie your dog say five or six feet from you, then to shoot the gun and after every shot to speak kindly to your dog and make him smell the gun. In a day or so repeat as before and the moment you see that your dog is not afraid let him loose and shoot again and always pet him. He will then know what a gun is. So when your young hound knows the gun, the canoe and water, he may be taught to be shy of strangers, traps and of poisoned baits.

To break a dog to hunt, you must not allow him to go in the bush whenever he likes. A dog that hunts without being in the company of his master will never be a well trained dog. Therefore, you must lead him in the bush and if you have a well trained dog, you may couple him with the young one and walk until you find a good trail then follow it with the dogs till you see that the young one has caught scent right, then let go the young hound first and the "old timer" last. If the hound comes from hunting stock, he will hang to the trail with the other dog and he will only turn up with him but for some reason or another, should the young hound come back to you, "don't get mad and kick or beat him." No, this is a great error and many are the dogs which have been spoiled that way. Instead of beating, speak kindly to him and pet him a few seconds and keep moving towards where the chase is going.

Don't excite your dog, pay no attention to him. If he wants to follow you at your heels, let him do so and once you reach a place where likely the other dog is going to pass, stay there and when the old dog comes along, the young one will again join and may stay this time with him, as the scent will be hot and the chances are ten to one that the young hound will take a hand in the music. But if after ten, or twenty minutes he should again return, treat him as before. Be always kind to him. If you have no old dog to train your young one, go with your dog and show him the game you want him to hunt, lead him until you kill one, then blood him. The blooding is the "A, B, C" of training. Allow him to smell the game all he likes, speak kindly to him even if he bites the game, don't kick him off or use a stick on him, as I have often seen done by some fellows who pretend that to teach a hound you must abuse him. If you want a foolish dog, that is the way to use him but if you desire an intelligent one, you must encourage him.

After a dog has been well blooded (the blooding is done by rubbing the hot blood of the game on the front legs, as well as on the sides of the dog), you may turn him loose or you may lead him until you find another trail. He will at once be anxious to follow. Let him lead for a hundred yards and once you are sure that he has the scent in the right direction, let him go and if that hound comes from trained stock, he will run that scent immediately and should he only be away for five, ten or more minutes and come back to you, speak kindly to him and tell him to hunt. Always mention his name and keep moving in the direction where you suppose the game is.

It is a good thing that a young dog backs his own tracks at first, as it teaches him that he can find you when he likes and a hound that does this after each chase will never get lost no matter where you may go. In deer hunting, it has many advantages in so far, that when you are several miles from camp, after your dog has a start you keep moving and if you find where a deer has just passed, you can just sit there and wait for the return of the dog and as soon as he returns, you just tie him and allow him to rest for fifteen or twenty minutes and then you start him again. I have often had two and sometimes four chases in one forenoon and this without bother. Hounds thus trained, will always return to camp every

Well Trained Hounds.

night for their feed and will be ready for the next day.

Some hunters say that their dogs are so good that when they turn them loose, they always stay away for three or four days and they even go so far as to say, that they hunt night and day during the whole time they are away. Well, this is not the case at all. The reason is that they will chase a deer or fox for three or four hours or more and when they have watered the deer or holed their fox, will then start to ramble around and start after another and after watering their second deer, they will be so far away that they are unable to find their way back, and they will walk until they can go no more. They will then lie down for a long time and walk around and howl until they find somebody's trail, which they will follow to the end or until they land at a settler's house or at some shanty and will remain there.

Now how many dogs like these will a party of ten or twelve men require to hunt, during ten or fifteen days in a strange country? When a hound has been away three or four days, is he in condition to run the next day after his return? No, it will take him as many days to recover and often he will be of no use for the remainder of the hunt.

Dogs like these may suit men living in the country where there is game. Their dogs after having been lost several times will, through time, know the lay of the country and be fairly good dogs at home, but take these hounds in a strange country, of what use and how many will a hunting party require to hunt every day of their outing? Well, they will require a car-load and be-

TRAINING THE DEER HOUND.

sides several men to hunt the dogs. Such dogs as these don't stay with me, as I consider them a nuisance, especially for city sportsmen, who are so busy during the whole year that they can only take a few weeks holiday every year, they require a strain of hounds on which they can depend every day of their hunt. I want a dog to be a flyer and to back track after every chase and to find me in the bush and not make for camp after his chase or wait at the shore until some "Johnny Sneakum" comes along with his canoe and says, "Get in Jack," and that Jack is only too glad to jump in and the next thing is that you don't see Jack for the balance of the season, but you will learn later on that Jack has been half starved that it will cost you $5.00 to $10.00 for the board if you desire to get Jack.

I will say here that I owe my life to two of my hounds. I was lost once in the woods in a blinding snow storm. This was in Western Ontario amongst a range of sappy pine hills. I was about five miles from camp. In the morning when I left the weather was very fine but it soon started to snow and the storm lasted until about 9 P. M. I was soaking wet and I had left my compass at camp, my matches were all wet and I slept in the bush. At 10 A. M. I had started my two hounds and about 11 A. M. they came back to me. It was just commencing to snow heavily but thinking it would not last long, I made for another hill where I was aware, if any deer started from there it was a sure run for our men, so I arrived there in due time and got a start. It was still snowing very heavily. I then pointed for home. I had about five miles more to reach our camp when I came to a place where a deer had just left his nest, so I thought that I could get a shot at him but after having followed him for about an hour, I gave him up and I tried to make for camp.

Well, instead of making for camp, I made a circle and came back to the same place where I had left the deer's track. It was 4 P. M., when my dogs came back to me. I knew then that I was completely turned so I decided to spend the night right there. I looked for a sheltered place and after removing all the snow I could I lay down with my back against a big flat stone and with my two dogs lying near me. We were quite comfortable and early in the morning, I pointed for camp. Now if these dogs had not returned to me, I really believe that I would not be able to write this, as their heat preserved me from freezing to death.

CHAPTER IX.

TRAINING — SPECIFIC THINGS TO TEACH.

TO teach the dog to bark treed, it is best, of course, to take him out with an old dog, but if you have no old dog, you can train him without one. This can be done by catching a live ground hog, 'coon or opossum. Take the animal you have to some small tree, a dogwood for instance, and let it climb from the ground up. It would be better if you could lead it or even drag it a short distance — ten feet, say, at first, to a tree.

Don't let your dog look on while doing this. After you have your animal treed, get your dog and bring him to the tree and give him the scent on the ground. If he is new at the business, he will not likely look up the tree, but will hunt for trail. If he finds where the animal is himself, try to get him to bark, but if he doesn't find it, then show him. Try to make him bark. That is one of the objects at this point as well as to find where the animal is.

Have your gun along, and as soon as you get your dog to bark, shoot into the air and at the same time, pull the animal out of the tree by the string by which he is tied. But whatever you do, don't let the animal get the best of your young dog or you will have a spoiled

Good Friends Get Along Best.

dog. I always liked a possum for this work because they are easy to handle and don't fight your dog.

SPECIFIC THINGS TO TEACH. 91

You must remember that, at this point, you are not training your dog to fight. The object is first to find where the animal goes and second to get your dog to "bark up." Continue this practice for some time; then put your animal in a larger tree out of sight but don't put in the same tree each time. After you have your dog trained so he will trail and bark up in the manner just described, the chances are that he will tree 'coon, if he gets a fresh trail. Of course, he will not be a good 'coon dog at once; that comes by experience.

Next to a good dog in the 'coon hunting business, is a good gun and lantern. Don't try to hunt 'coon with a common open lantern. A good kind of lantern to find their eyes with is a dark or police lantern, as you don't have to put them on your head to find their eyes. But whatever kind you use, have one with a good bullseye and a reflector. Use a good shot gun. I generally use No. 2 shot.

Having prepared ourselves with a good dog, gun and lantern, we are now ready for business. We will go out first on a cloudy night. We will go into the woods and walk slowly, giving the dog plenty of time to hunt and if we don't see him pretty soon, we will sit down on a log and wait a while.

Don't go thru the woods as if some one were

after you or as if you were in a hurry and then call your dog as soon as you get thru the woods. You will never have a good 'coon dog if you do so, especially if he is new at the business. If you want a dog that will stay by the trail, you want to stay with him. If you use your dog properly, that is, if you hunt slow and sit down on a log or wait for your dog until he comes in and then move on as soon as he does come in, you will find that your dog will soon "catch on" to this and will always come in as soon as he has a woods or a portion of a woods hunted over, unless he "trees."

Another brother offers the following suggestions: "Let me give you a few pointers in regard to breaking them to hunt 'coon. When the pup is five or six months old, teach him to speak or bark by holding up a piece of meat or bread, and when you get him so he will bark, take him into the woods where there are squirrels. Be sure and take your gun along and chase every squirrel or cat up a tree and shoot the squirrel. Be sure and make the dog help to chase the squirrel then skin the squirrel. Cut it up in small pieces and feed it to your dog. Do this as often as possible and you will be surprised how quickly he will learn. Commence early in the fall to hunt 'coon, and keep away as much as possible from the haunts of the rabbit with your dog, but if he gets after a rabbit, get him off as soon as possible and scold him. I wouldn't advise anyone to hunt rabbits with dog until thoroughly broken to hunt 'coon."

TEACHING THE DOG HOW TO SWIM.

As for swimming, we are aware that all dogs when thrown in the water can swim, but the question is, will they swim right and take to water at once. I say no, they all need training before they will take to water when told, swim and float right and remain in the water for hours when necessary, and also return game from water when required whether it be for fur or feathers.

To teach a dog to swim, take him often to a nice shore and let him play at the edge of the water and say nothing to him. After you have done this during three or four days, tie him and row about thirty yards from shore. Use a flat bottom boat or a good safe one and place him gently in the water, hold his head above the water till he floats, then row to the shore. He will follow and as soon as you land, get out of the boat and call him to the shore. This will teach him to land because should you stay in the boat, he will try to get in the boat with you.

Now allow him to play for five or ten minutes, then repeat the same tactics but row a little further. After two or three days lessons such as these, the dog will take the water. To make him do this, row a few yards from the shore and call him. He will at once follow you. Row slowly away and the moment you see he is getting tired, pull him on board or row to shore. Never train your dog to swim during cold weather but when it is warm and sunny. A nice sunny morning is the best time to teach them to swim. Once he knows how to swim right, take him across a small river or lake and then come back and make him swim back. He will then never be afraid of water.

To teach a hound to properly ride in a canoe, tie him and have a whip or a small switch and make him lie down. Always speak to him kindly. Mention the dog's name and say lie down. If he does not obey, whip but do so carefully. "Avoid whipping," because there has been many dogs that would have been good hunters that have been completely spoiled by the whip. Always speak to your dog, then give one single stroke; if he does not obey give another stroke and so on until he does so. As soon as he lies down, you can allow him to put up his head and look above the boat and row across the river or lake. Once on the other

SPECIFIC THINGS TO TEACH. 95

side, order him off and hold your rope which must be a long one. If he goes to jump, give him a good check and make him walk off easily. Once he is landed, hold him and pet him. Stay there five minutes or so, then get in the boat again, hold the boat and order your dog to get in the boat. I use the word "Board." Mention the dog's name and say "board" and to order him out, say "move."

As soon as the dog gets in the boat say, "Lie down" or just "down" and if he does not obey, show him the whip and command him, then whip. As soon as he is down, get in and row a few hundred yards further and repeat the same a dozen of times. The moment the dog obeys, you must pet him so as to make him understand that what he does is right. If you will repeat the same tactics for three or four days, the dog will soon know how to balance himself and will be very steady — you will never have any bother with him. Thus a dog trained to water and canoe is a very handy thing for you as well as for the dog. Should you have no room in the canoe, he will swim. If you have room, just for him he will be as safe for you to take on board as a stone. A pair of hounds so trained will just balance your canoe right. It is a good thing to put some hay, straw or a bag in the bottom of the boat or canoe for the dog to lie down on. They will soon know their place to lay.

A QUICK METHOD.

Having many years of experience in the breeding and training of hounds to hunt nearly all kind of game, a Canadian brother hunter tells how to train dogs for 'coon when he has no old dog to teach the young one.

1st. Set a trap where you see 'coon signs as follows: Take the skin or part of a good sized green codfish, tie it to a string and drag it along the bank of a creek or place where you see their signs, to the place you wish to set your trap.

2nd. Take a good sized stick about 4 feet long, drive it well on a nice flat piece of land, then tie what you have dragged to this stick about 20 inches from the ground. Have the bait well tied so that Mr. 'Coon will have a hard job to pull a piece off.

3rd. Take three No. 1½ or larger size steel traps, but not very stiff spring, set them 8 inches from the stick and arrange in such a way as to form a triangle. Have the chains well secured so that Mr. 'Coon will only be caught in one of the traps. Dig holes for four traps and cover chain and traps with dry grass or leaves. Be careful not to put anything to interfere with the jaws of your traps and make things look as natural as possible. Visit your traps the next morning and the chances will be that you will have one or two 'coons waiting you. I have often found three waiting me in one setting as above. When you have a coon or two, take one at a time to an open field about 400 yards from the bush, then tie a long clothes line to the ring of the chain in such a way that it will not slip off. At the other end of the line, tie something white, and allow Mr. 'Coon to make for the bush. Have a friend with you that will keep an eye on Mr. 'Coon. Then take your dog to the spot in the field where the coon started from, and make him take the scent, and once he has it in the right direction and commences to pull, turn him loose and follow him.

If the hound comes from good stock, he will soon find Mr. 'Coon and will bark at him. Encourage him and have your friend pull on the line in order to make the 'coon move. The dog will then catch him; after the hound has pinched the 'coon a couple of times, throw the line over a branch of some good sized tree and help the 'coon to climb. Allow the dog to bark for a while. Shoot the coon, open him at once and blood your dog well by rubbing the blood on his front legs and over his body.

If you have another coon, repeat the same

with the second as you have done with the first, but in another direction of the field and bush. Always allow the 'coon to go far enough so that your dog will not see him. When you take him where the coon scent is, after the 'coon is dead and your dog well blooded, go home with your dog and 'coon. Chain your dog and put the 'coon near him for three or four hours before skinning and while doing this, have your dog near you. The next day, take your dog where 'coons are moving and he will soon have one for you. Repeat the blooding every time and you will soon have a No. 1 'coon dog.

TRAINING—RANDOM SUGGESTIONS, ETC. 99

Co-operation Between the Man and His Dogs Brings Results.

CHAPTER X.

TRAINING — RANDOM SUGGESTIONS FROM MANY SOURCES.

SUMMING up we find much pointed and valuable information relating to the training of dogs omitted thru lack of space. From this we present a chapter of "nuggets" in paragraph form, which will no doubt prove interesting and beneficial to those interested in training hunting dogs. Here are a few things not to do:

Don't allow your dogs to run into every farmyard as you pass along the road.

Don't allow them to be used with which to run stock.

Don't let them get into the habit of running other dogs.

Don't let them run house-cats.

Don't teach him to be called by shooting.

Don't, when out hunting, keep urging him all the time.

Don't let every one have him to hunt with or he will soon be everybody's dog.

Don't allow them to come into the house and get into every pan and kettle, if your wife is good-natured.

Don't correct him by pulling his ears, for a fox dog needs his hearing.

Don't feed but twice a day, and don't stint him on his feed before starting on a race.

Don't allow him to run loose when you are not using him.

* * *

Did you ever try using a sheep bell on a still trailer on windy, stormy nights? It's a suc- bells on sheep and disregard them until the dog but 'coon usually become accustomed to sheep bells on sheep and disregards them until the dog gets too close for them to escape. Then, where not accustomed to the bell, their curiosity overcomes their fear. The best pair of 'coon dogs I ever owned was Sport, a fox hound and collie, half and half, a slow semi-mute trailer, and Simon, a full blood fox terrier, a fast mute trailer. I used a bell on Sport. This and his occasional barks on the trail kept the attention of the 'coon while Simon cut across lots and invariably took him unawares.

I have learned at considerable expense that the best at most any price is the cheapest. If you want a good, cheap 'coon dog, get a half pup collie and half fox hound. Never give him a taste of nor let him see a rabbit, teach him a few tricks (to make him pay for his meals), such as jumping over a stick, then a pole, then a fence. This is to teach him to obey every word.

Never scold or whip him, gain his confidence, teach him to speak for bits of meat so when the time comes to hunt 'coon you can get him to bark up; get him to catch and carry and he will often catch an opossum or maybe a mink or 'coon and kill it when away from you, and if you teach him to bring everything (rats, woodchucks) home to you, he will do the same in the woods after night. Never let him get whipped by another dog or woodchuck, 'coon or even a big rat. Always help him kill or whip everything he jumps on to or that jumps on to him. A defeat will discourage him.

When your young dog is ready for a night hunt in the woods or cornfield, choose the best and most favorable night for the first trip. Feed no meat nor milk for 24 hours previous to the first or any subsequent trip, for that matter, for the best dogs, full of meat or milk, cannot do good work on the most favorable night. Feed him a good dinner of vegetables, but no supper until you return from the hunt, then give him anything. Choose a dark and cloudy night, the darker the better, not too still, as usually on very still nights the atmosphere is heavy and smoke settles to the earth, so likewise does the scent of the 'coon trail, and many a fine dog has

TRAINING — RANDOM SUGGESTIONS, ETC. 103

been condemned for failing to locate his 'coon when started under such a condition as this.

* * *

Do not return home and leave your hounds in the woods, rather walk a mile or two to catch them and they will be in better shape to hunt the next day than if you had allowed them to run all night.

* * *

I notice so many of the boys in telling of their 'coon hunting say when Old Jack or Trailer, or whatever his name might be, strikes a trail they follow him as fast as they can run until out of wind, then as soon as he barks treed, they go to him on the double quick, over logs, brush, barb wire fences, thru brier patches, swamps and so on. Now, this may be all right, I am not condemning any one else's method of hunting, but just want to exchange ideas. When my dog strikes a trail or I have reason to think there is anything doing, I just wait right where I am until they tree or come back to me. If they bark treed, I just take my time and if I know of a way around that will save going thru some thicket or up some very steep hill, I just go around and save those hardships. And another thing I never do is whoop and hallo at my dogs when they are working. I think that has spoiled many a good dog, and never run to a dog as soon as he barks up, but give him time to think it over and circle the tree a few times; then, when he settles down again you can go to him and depend upon the 'coon being there.

PART II.

BREEDING AND CARE OF DOGS.

106   HUNTING DOGS.

Some Ideals.

CHAPTER XI.

SELECTING THE DOG.

DIFFERENT hunters have different ideas as to the style of dog best suited to their purposes. We can only approach the subject, by giving views of experienced breeders, and the reader may choose as he is inclined.

From a Canadian Hunter comes the following:

This question of the right kind of dogs to select is a matter on which many sportsmen differ in opinion. Some prefer the small, some the medium and others the large hound. For me I like a hound to be from 24 to 27 inches high at the shoulder and well put together, with a lot of bones, straight front legs with strong and compact feet, "but not too large" with good strong nails well set in, the body to be long and not short of flank with a wide chest and a moderate deep chest and with a strong broad back, hind legs with the right kind of bend, that is neither straight or too much curved in, with well furnished thighs.

Dogs with straight hind legs cannot run and

jump over logs and fences with the same ease as those having a marked bend. These dogs can buckle and unbuckle with more quickness and power, such as is required in the gallop than dogs having a round barrel shaped chest, with both the front and hind legs straight. Dogs having a nearly round chest cannot stand any length of hard running, such as those having a narrow chest because a dog with a moderate deep and narrow chest has better wind as he is able to alter the cubic contents of his chest more rapidly and thus inhale and expire a larger volume of air. Therefore, a dog with a deep or flat chest will always have a greater speed than one with a round one. This is a well known fact in all animals remarkable for their speed, such as deer, wolf and greyhound.

I like dogs with good muscular thighs with a fine long tapering and graceful wavering stern, ears to be well set and not too long and not thick and slabby, neck to be long and well set between the shoulders, the head and muzzle, this is only a matter of taste. Those I prefer are those having a long and narrow forehead and a fairly square muzzle, ears from 7 to 9 inches long, lips loose but not hanging low, throat loose and roomy in the skin and a good coat of hair so they can stand cold and water, and with a good loud tongue and keen nose. The color has nothing to

SELECTING THE DOG.

do, the main point is the staying quality, the speed, scent and endurance; the intelligence and the particular style of ranging or beating the ground for trail as well as to run it once found, with great speed.

Some say a fine looking hound should be a good hunter. Well, any hunter of experience in the handling of hounds is fully aware that it is not always the dog which carries the prizes at the shows that is the best dog in the field. The same thing exists with the horse. Some people claim that it all depends on the breeding, others on the training. The fact is that both are required as well as the right shape the dog should have to be able to stand hard work day after day.

* * *

The most essential thing to the value and working capabilities of fox hounds is purity of blood, declares another. Too much care, therefore, cannot be taken in selecting and breeding fox hounds. Hounds for running the red fox should be selected from the best possible blood that can be obtained. I like a hound with a long clear voice — one that can be heard at least two miles away on an ordinary calm day — and one that gives tongue freely when running and trailing but not one that gives tongue when he has run over the trail and lost scent.

* * *

In selecting a night hunting dog I prefer one that is three-quarters or at least one-half fox hound. The reason is, the fox hound has a good nose, also a good voice and speed. While I do not condemn a dog that is bred in any other way, I prefer one bred as I have stated for the reasons given above.

Some prefer a dog that is part beagle, but if any reader of this book has ever tried to train a dog with good beagle blood in his veins to hunt coon, he has been up against the real thing. The trouble is, the beagle has it bred right in him to run rabbits, and blood will tell. The only point in favor of the beagle is his nose. With the exception of the bird dog the beagle has the finest scent of the whole dog family. I know this to be true by observation. A fox gives off more scent than a rabbit, so does a coon and all the other animals.

During the "nesting season" birds give scarcely any. This is a wise provision of Nature to protect them from their enemies during this important period.

One day I saw a fine English setter almost step on a grouse that was sitting on her nest. He never scented her until she went whirling out the ridge right in front of his nose. That dog's actions told more plainly than words could have done, how deeply he regretted the incident.

SELECTING THE DOG. 111

I have also seen a beagle run a rabbit after a heavy rain, the rabbit, to my knowledge, having run before the rain fell.

* * *

Many writers say that a dog's pedigree and his being registered, does not amount to the paper it is written on. Now I do not wish to criticise any of my brother sportmen, but I think it is the only way to know if one's dog is well bred, and to have a well bred dog means much less trouble in training him. Do not get discouraged if your dog does not train as easily as he should, and always remember that much depends upon you. Stay with your dog if you want him to be a good sticker. Many a dog has been spoiled by leaving him to run for nothing.

In selecting a dog to hunt all kinds of game, get a good bred hound. I have no use for mongrels or curs. They are dear at any price. Get a thick, hard, round-footed, long ears coming out of head low down, well developed chest, shortish tail, large at root or next to body, long from hip to gamble joint, with broad strong back, wide nostrils and long pendant lip. Now this is my idea of a good all around hunting dog. I don't expect you to find all of these qualifications in any one dog.

* * *

Have decided that for my use, a full blooded

hound. That is a good, fast and reliable trailer, one that will stay with the trail, cold or hot, and never think of giving up until asked to. One that will bark treed on a cold trail just the same as if he had run him up a sight chase. One that should he in cold trailing run across a hot trail and tree, will after catching go and take up cold trail again and tree.

* * *

When it comes to large hounds for coon, fox, etc., a cross of the right kind of American fox hounds and the right kind of blood hounds fills the bill to perfection. The blood hound has the keenest scent of any dog living. The American fox hound has the speed. If a man has a combination of the two he is starting on the right trail. I prefer a fox hound bitch bred to bloodhound dog. How many ever saw a thoroughbred bloodhound? They are a heavy built hound, medium size heavy head, long ears, square deep muzzle, with heavy rolls of wrinkles on head just over the eyes, which gives him a surly look. I have seen what were called and sold for bloodhounds to a sheriff to trail man. They would trail fairly well, but they came a long ways from being thoroughbred bloodhounds. Any hound trained when young can be taught to trail man or beast.

Hunters differ as to the kind of dog to use

SELECTING THE DOG.

for coon hunting. The best coon dog I ever had (and I've had a good many) was a half Scotch terrier and I don't know what the other half was. He was black and white spotted with curly hair and weighed but thirty-two pounds.

Some hunters prefer the shepherd dog and again some would hunt with nothing else but a hound. I don't know as it makes much difference what kind of a dog one uses, just so it is one of the hunting kind, a good trailer and thoroughly well trained. Of course, not every dog, even of the hunting kind, will make a good coon dog; about the only way to tell is to try.

* * *

As to picking a pup for a coon hound, it is very hard to do, but I want a full bloodhound, one that tongues on trail and a free barker at tree. I want the old style hound, as the modern fox hounds are too nervous for good coon hounds, although you may get one once in a while that will work a cold trail very well.

A cross between the old style, long eared hound and the fast trailing hound with large, heavy shoulders, deep chest, a large fore leg, large broad head, long ears, rather short coupled back, slightly roached back, with a good square nose, rather large neck, set well down in the shoulders. While this is my kind of hound for coon, do not understand me to say that I want an extra slow trailer, for I do not, but I want him to be steady, and when he has a trail he can work it fast. This is my kind of a dog for coon, but he would not be in it with an up to date fox hound on a fox chase, but running fox and coon are different, and I want a different kind of a hound.

* * *

We have made a success in raising bear hounds, and find the only way to get a good pup with the hunting habit, is to have it bred in them first, says a California Brother. One has to have good parent hounds, and while the mother dog is carrying the pups she must be worked on whatever you want your pups to run. For instance, we have a black and tan long eared bitch, bred her to a good hound, one quarter stag. Before she had these puppies we caught three bears with others, letting her get in and fight hard.

These puppies when a month old would crawl on a bear hide rug, chew and shake at it, and when three months old, would track, bark and fight. Now they are five months old and know considerable about it. We treed an old bear, and these pups kept right on and treed two cubs, and barked up and stayed until we found them after we had the old one skinned and cut up. They have the instinct in them, and are beauties with just enough stag in them to have a good crop of whiskers.

Embryo Trailers.

CHAPTER XII.

CARE AND BREEDING.

AS we must raise the dog before concerning ourselves with his culture, let us begin with the pup.

I commence to care for the pups by giving the bitch plenty of exercise before they are born. Then as soon as they are born, put them in a clean, dry place, where they will be comfortable, — if in winter, where cold winds cannot reach them; if in summer, in a cool place out of the hot sun. Feed the bitch well on good food of different varieties; do not chain her, but rather shut her up in a park of something of the kind, where she can exercise but not get out to run, for if she should run she gets hot and you may loose some if not all of your puppies.

By the time the pups are three weeks old, you will need to commence feeding some milk twice each day, gradually increasing the amount as the bitch becomes dry, and when she weans them, feed three times a day, until about six months old; after which I only feed twice a day.

In this connection we quote from an article in a current magazine, the truth of the conten-

CARE AND BREEDING. 117

tions being borne out to a greater or less extent by our own observations:

After her puppies are about five weeks of age a bitch will begin to vomit the contents of her stomach for the puppies. I have known many breeders of experience argue that but few bitches do so. Over and over again have I been able to convince persons who, having immediate care of the bitch and her litter, deny that the bitch ever vomits to her puppies, that they are wrong. Many bitches never vomit when the attendant is about, and only appear to do so at night; hence the belief that they do not do so at all. It is the natural manner in which the bitch feeds her whelp with partially digested food, after her milk supply ceases to suffice for their requirements. If the bitch is of good constitution and in good health, the puppies flourish remarkably on the diet thus provided, and in such cases my experience leads me to believe that puppies left with their dams do better than when separated from them and, strange to say, bitches who are in the habit of picking up all sorts of apparently undesirable odds and ends do not seem to do their puppies less well under these circumstances than cleaner feeders do.

Many bitches eat the young soon as they come if not closely watched, especially the first time. There should be an attendant at time of whelping. Whelps must be removed to a basket of warm cloths and kept away till all have come and then place to matron for nursing. There is no danger of her devouring them thereafter.

To resume: This is what I feed pups: grind rye without bolting and sometimes oats ground very fine; then run through a coarse sieve, and bake into bread without soda or baking powder, or make into a thick mush and feed it with plenty of milk if convenient. As they grow older add cornmeal and scraps from the butcher shop to the feed, and give them enough to keep them nice and sleek, but do not overfeed.

By the time they are three weeks old they will be running everywhere, and let them have plenty of room to run and play. Change their beds as often as needed, which is a good way to prevent fleas. Should fleas get on them as they are sure to do, put a tablespoonful of oil of tar in a quart of warm water, take a fine tooth comb, dip in tar water, and comb them until the hair is thoroughly saturated; repeating as often as needed.

For bedding, the best is leaves from the woods; straw will answer, but I prefer the leaves to anything I have ever tried, but whatever is used it should be changed often and kept dry. For the dog with a damp place to sleep, will soon have the mange, and it is far easier to keep a dog healthy than to cure him after he has become diseased. In warm weather I use no bedding as it is only a harbor for vermin.

The best place by far, to keep your dogs, is in a park, where there is shade in summer, with running water, and slope enough to the land, to allow it to be well washed whenever it rains. Then provide dry, comfortable quarters to sleep, and you have an ideal home for dogs. In case you cannot have a place of this kind nor even a small park, and must keep your dog chained, attach a good heavy wire to the dog house and the other end to a tree, where your dog can get to a shade if possible; then attach a chain to the wire so your dog can travel along the wire; but be sure that he cannot get tangled up and have to lay out some wet night

Some are situated far better than others for taking care of dogs and I am sorry to say there is an occasional sportsman (or at least he owns a dog or two), who is inclined to let his dogs shift for themselves. I pity the dog that is unfortunate enough to have such an owner.

My experience is that too much meat is not good for the foxhound, and if they get a mess of old stale meat just before you want to run them, the chances are that they can't make the race. I have seen good dogs that couldn't run an hour, simply because they were filled up with old dead hog or horse. If you want to make a good race with your dog, keep him tied two or three days before you intend to run him, feed him corn bread (well baked) and sweet milk. If you run at night, give your dog a good feed at noon and very little at night when you start, and if your hound has the "stuff" in him he is good for all night.

It think rotten meat will affect the smelling of a dog as well as heat them up, so they can't make a good race. To let your dog run loose until you are ready for a chase, where he can find slop and such stuff to be filled up on, and have your friend meet you with his hounds in fine shape and lead your hound all the time, well you know how you would feel.

Some say you must have it bred in a hound to run. That is all true enough, but a well bred hound with all grit can't make a good race if he isn't in shape to do it.

The foregoing is borne out and added detail given in the following contribution from New York State:

I find that fox hounds which I feed on old stinking pork or stinking meat of any kind are quite stupid and very careless about hunting. They cannot keep on the trail, neither do they wish to run fast or continue running long. Old

CARE AND BREEDING. 121

stinking pork seems to be the worst I could feed to a fox hound, and corn bread and some milk on it seems to be the best.

When my dogs are fed on cornbread and milk they display the most activity, and can follow a fox or rabbit more accurately and accordingly run faster. When I want to make my hound run slow I feed him some meat, and the more it stinks the less he can smell anything but the fumes of this in his stomach. I can easily tell by the smell of my dog's breath whether he has eaten fresh mutton or rotten horse recently, and I think any healthy person can easily.

Here are another hunter's views on this same subject:

In rearing hounds, to have them hardy and intelligent you must feed them right and provide them with a lot of good fresh water as well as to give them daily exercise. When I feed beef, I have a small axe with which I chop all the bones into fine pieces. They also get scraps from the table with some vegetables mixed with cooked rolled oats. I feed the old ones once a day with raw meat and once with porridge. I see that they get just enough to keep them always in good running condition, that is neither fat nor thin. I like a dog with a good rolling skin. I never take a skeleton dog in the woods as I have often seen hunters going deer hunting with dogs which you could read a newspaper through.

Now of what use are such animals as these? Some say that a thin dog will run better than a fat one. Yes, if the fat one is hog fat; but a dog with about one-half inch of hard fat on the ribs will out-do a dozen of these starved dogs of which you can count the bones at one hundred yards from them. No, a dog with just the skin and bones cannot stand any work for the reason that he has no bottom.

Young pups should be fed at the very least three times daily, four times is still better. Never give them more than what they can eat, and in the meantime see that they just get enough so as to clean the dish well at every meal and in no case should the pan containing the food be left in the intervals with the puppies if they have not cleaned it out as they will become disgusted with it and next time refuse to feed. Keep everything clean and dry and always feed at the same hour daily. It is much easier to rear a pair of pups than a single one.

Before weaning the dew-claw should always be removed. These are of no use but only serve to bother the dogs and hounds should always have them cut off.

Worm medicine should always be given to

all young dogs and kennels should be lime washed at least three times a year and never allow your dogs to sleep near the stove and then turn them out in the cold. If you desire a lazy hound allow him to burn himself at the stove, out if on the contrary you wish a lively dog, provide him with a good dry kennel and if you keep several dogs see that each one has his own stall. This has the advantage of preventing them from fighting and from the risk of taking cold by lying out of the kennel.

When your dogs return from the hunt always examine their feet and legs and if you find any sore spots attend to them at once. If the dogs return wet to camp always allow them to dry near a stove before turning them to their kennel which should be a good dry one.

If you desire your dogs to stand hard work day after day you must look after them with as much care as a jockey attends to his horse.

The very moment you notice your dog is looking dull ascertain at once what is the cause, and if you are of the opinion that it is a cold or distemper, don't wait until you see his eyes and nose running, to doctor him, but attend to him immediately.

A Pair of Young Coonhounds.

CHAPTER XIII.

BREEDING.

THE main and most important question in breeding race horses as well as hounds is to get always the very best and to do this, one has to be on the move and watch the hunting and staying quality as well as the style of looking for trails, etc.; and a breeder should always be ready to pay the price for a good sire or dam. And he should always bear in mind that there is no more trouble or bother and that it does not cost more to raise a pair of dogs from well known hunting stock than from unknown stock but where it tells is when the dogs are of age for training. It is here where the great difference exists and where a sportsman is willing to look at the right side of the matter finds his mistake and where he regrets not having paid a few dollars more for the right stock.

Some say that if pedigreed dogs were trained they would beat the other dogs. The question is to train them. Hounds which come from untrained or from partly or badly trained stock will always be poor hunters. They will never be the dogs that they would have been had they come from highly trained stock, that is that their sire and dam and grand sire and grand dam were all trained by persons who thoroughly understood the way of breeding and rearing as well as the age and proper way of training. A hound coming from such selected stock will learn and pick up in a day what will take others months and probably a whole season to learn. I never kept a hound which after having shown him the game and also blooded him once or twice would not at once start to hunt because I consider that the sooner a sportsman will shoot such dogs the better.

There are plenty of fox dogs that are good coon dogs, and a great many coon dogs will run a fox to a finish, but the fox and coon dogs are two very different dogs. There is also a greater difference in the opinions of hunters, in regard to the coon dog than in any other dogs.

Some want the full blooded hound, and some a cross with a foxhound; here they differ again as to what dog to cross with; others want no hound blood at all, but a shepherd; one wants a collie and another just a dog. Then here is a hunter who insists on a silent dog; and the next one says the silent trailer doesn't camp with him.

Now as I am not looking for trouble, I will agree with all of you. Where coons are plenti-

BREEDING.

ful and you are likely to strike a coon track in every cornfield, the half hound or even a cur dog, will get coons; but where they are scarce and you may tramp until near morning, and then strike a trail five or six hours old, if you get that coon, you will need a dog with a good nose and one that tongues on a trail. But there is one point on which you will all agree — if your dog does not stay at a tree and bark good and plenty, he isn't much of a coon dog. Consequently in breeding for coon dogs, this is the most important point. Get as many other coon points as you can, but be sure his ancestors have been good tree dogs, as far back as you can trace them.

The very reason that there are so many culls in this country, is because many hunters think a dog is a dog, and that any dog with long ears is a hound. Ears count for nothing but looks; bent legs, ditto; the only way that you can perfect the breed, which in your estimation, is the ideal, is by choosing the dogs of the best particular kind which you prefer. For instance, how could a hunter expect to produce a strain of dogs with good, loud voices, if he chooses as his breeders the poorest squallers in the lot? Nature is nature, and it is only by studying her laws that we are able to produce our ideal of any kind; also, if he wants an intelligent dog, he must pick out the one with the most desired good points, and then he is on the fair way to success.

In short, in order to have a hound that will repay you for his training, he must be bred right in every detail or the hunter is doomed to disappointment. If the hunter does not own a first class pair to breed from and cannot secure a good strain in his locality, he should buy from a reliable dealer, one whom he knows has made a success of breeding this class of dogs. It is also advisable to buy a young pup as the chances of securing the best are alike to all, or even though the parent dogs are No. 1 in every respect, there will be some in the litter that will be weak in points before they have reached the age of eight months, the breeder himslf will have difficulty in choosing any one as the best.

There is a standard for judging the so-called high class pedigree show dogs but which does not cut much ice with a fox and coon hunter. Regardless of color, the qualities most desirable in an all around fox hound are: 1st, staying qualities and powers of endurance. 2d, voice, feet and general make up.

Personally, I like a hound that stands from 20 to 24 inches at shoulder, long in body, deep chested, heavy boned with a coat of rather long hair, the feet should be round in shape with a

BREEDING

good covering of hair to protect the soles or pads. A foxhound should not have a second claw on the hind leg for ehis shows a cross in his breeding. A dog that has these claws will not stand much hard running in crust for by rubbing against trees, etc., they will gradually become sore and bleeding, and the hound although willing enough is handicapped with a pair of sore legs. Some hunters cut these claws off while young. In the pure strain of fox dogs this would be unnecessary as they would not have them on.

The first cost of a young hound is nothing compared with the time and trouble it takes to bring him to a hunting age. Therefore, it is advisable to buy the best obtainable for even though the price be high at first cost, the hunter will be better satisfied for his time and money when the dog has fully developed for the chase. In making a choice for breeding, select a pair that has been thoroughly tried and are known to have no weak points, such as poor voice, quitters, back trackers, etc. It is also advisable to hunt with the bitch as much as possible up to the very time the pups are whelped. The pups will be stronger and better in every way than if the mother had been housed in all the time and a hunter will find that a pup so bred will take to hunting almost as soon as he can run.

HUNTING DOGS.

Do not breed a pair of young dogs, rather select if possible, an old dog for a young bitch for by breeding two young dogs their pups are apt to be hot-headed, over-anxious and these qualities are not wanted in a foxhound.

To be sure of a strain of dogs the breeder must know their ancestors three generations back for it is surprising how far back a pup will breed from, not only in color but in characteristics, habits, etc.

Fox Hounds.

A Nice Pack of Hunting Dogs.

CHAPTER XIV — BREEDING (Continued).

Crossing for Coon Dogs.

MY experience has been that the crossing of an English pointer dog and American fox hound slut for 'coon dogs, are the best I ever saw, writes an Ohio night hunter of rare judgment and experience, and I will illustrate by relating the accomplishments of a certain dog of the breeding. I will say further that the sire of this dog I mention was the most remarkable I ever heard of — a fine large pointer, and often when hunting quails or pheasants in the woods he would bark up and had done it many times before they found out the cause.

One day while hunting pheasants he began to bark up a hollow beech stub, and when called, refused to leave his post, and his hair was slightly raised, which excited the hunter's curiosity and they procured an axe and felled the stub. To their surprise, two large 'coons came rolling out and were dispatched. This solved the problem, and after that, he was the cause of many 'coons losing their life, as he located them in the den and trees where they had not stepped a foot on the ground. I for one can surely recommend this cross to make good 'coon dogs.

* * *

A few points in regard to a stud dog for fox. Pick a dog with a deep chest, good strong loin, long head and stands with his feet well under him. About the feet — take the foot in your hand, press gently, and if it feels firm and springy like a piece of rubber, that dog has a good foot, which is very necessary in a fox dog, but if he has a soft, mushy foot, let that dog alone, no matter how good he looks, for he will not stand long chases, and the old adage that like begets like, will surely show itself in this case.

* * *

There are a great many worthless dogs, but the dogs are not to blame. I am writing on fox dogs, but it holds good on all dogs. There is always a worthless bitch, and sometimes several of them to be had for nothing, and some fellow who wants a dog but don't want to pay a fair price says, "I'll get that bitch and breed her to that dog down at Graysville. They say he's a crackerjack, and I'll get some good dogs and they won't cost me anything either."

Well, when the time comes to breed it's

BREEDING (CONTINUED).

five miles to Graysville, and the roads are awful muddy, and he concluded to breed to Jim Jones' dog just over the way, saying he ain't much of a dog, and a cousin to the bitch, but his great-grandmother got more foxes than any dog over in these parts, and some of the pups will breed back. He gets eight or ten pups, which he gets perhaps $1.00 a piece for, and it costs just as much to raise a poor one as a good one. The owners spend a lot of time trying to make dogs of them and have nothing at last.

In a running dog these are the qualities I think are needed. First, endurance, because no dog can make a race after a red fox without it. Then speed, a good nose, lots of ambition, good sense and the more of that the better; and will need to be able to hear well to enable him to cut corners if he happens to get behind, as any dog is liable to do.

After the pups are born, don't let the bitch run until they are weaned, for it will hurt both mother and puppies. Should she get very hot and then get to her pups you would likely lose some or perhaps all of them.

Here we have still another favorite breed for 'coon hunting, advanced by an old and tried hunter. Says he: My choice of a breed of 'coon dog is a grade hound crossed on a bull or one-half hound, one fourth rat terrier and one-fourth Scotch collie or shepherd or fox hound and beagle.

Says another: A hound to be a fine ranger does not require many years of training if he comes from a sire and dam that were both good rangers and which their own sire and dam and grand sire and grand dam were all good and highly trained dogs. He is sure to hang from them and any sportsman having dogs of that strain will enjoy the use of his dog at once, but where it takes three or five seasons and sometimes more to make a good dog, is when they come from exhibition stock or from stock that have never been broken right. If a hound is wrongly taught to hunt he will always be a crazy dog and will, if bred, give poor hunters exactly like himself.

An Ohio Fox Hunter goes on record thus: In breeding hounds some seem to expect great work on any line they wish to see the hound, not stopping to think everything to its kind and everything to be perfect must be true to his nature. The bloodhound is true to his nature with reasonable opportunity. He is a man trailer, a large, strong dog, built for strength and endurance but not for fleetness which all breeders concede the 'coon dog should be built upon. Strong in my opinion with strong jaws,

BREEDING (CONTINUED).

good size and a good muzzle, a good scent with as much speed and determination as you can inject into their blood.

I am now speaking of coon dogs. They may be bred almost any way and yet be good coon dogs but I find it is just as necessary to have them bred from coon hunting stock as for any dog or animal to be trained for any specific or especial purpose. It must be bred with that object in view and as much of that blood and disposition injected into the veins as is possible to get.

The fox hound is a special or specific type or breed of dog. He is bred for it, built for it, trained for it and if a true type of hound, is it. Not all well bred dogs are fox dogs nor are all well bred horses fast. Only one in many. But in order to have grounds to expect speed, we must have breeding, as the saying goes, "Blood will tell." Some are daffy on pedigree, others must have everything registered, others ask only for the swing and staying qualities of their ancestors, etc.

All breeds of hounds have some worthless, yet some may be fairly good along some particular line and very much at fault in others. Some have speed but cannot be got to use it, will not get in with a pack and run to a finish. Some will run with a slow pack all right but put them in with a fast pack and they will have their gallop out in from one to two hours. They seem to have all the courage necessary but not the speed. Some will go after the first fox trail they ever smell of and others you have to train to follow.

I think this difference largely between the dog that is allowed to run at large and one raised in a corral. One is fearful of everything, the other fearless and full of self-confidence. Confidence is worth much in both dog and man. So many cannot run unless they have their noses directly over the trail and have no driving instinct. If they lose the trail, go back and get it and bring it up to where they lost it before. So for several times, perhaps, before getting away, the dog running all the time, Mr. Fox sitting down waiting, resting. You never hear of such dogs catching or holding a fox. They seem to be willing but lack the tact and fox sense.

I would say to breeders there are only a few characteristics necessary for good foxhounds and every breeder should see to this with careful study and tests. First — Courage. Do not breed a dog on either side that has not got it. It will crop out to make you ashamed of your dog some time. Second — Speed. It is just as natural for the lover of a chase to want to be ahead, as for the lover of the horse race, but we cannot all be so; often we find it easy to beat

BREEDING (CONTINUED) 139

our slow packs in the neighborhood and how we swell up and think we can best anybody until we get away from home and get that bubble pricked.

Other qualifications as to form and shape. A dog should be compact enough to be strong. He should be just as long as he can be to gather quickly. A dog too long turning on all kinds of ground is like a horse with a very long stride trying to go fast on a short track. His stride is too long for the lay of the ground. Another qualification and not in the least, — is voice. The dog that has no voice holds not the highest place in his owner's pride. A good hound, one prized by his owner and loved by the lover of the chase must do three things at once, run fast, carry the trail and tongue well. These requisitions make a good fox dog and if his shape and symmetry is good, he is a valued dog.

Breeders should look to it that these qualities are bred for at the sacrifice of everything else. There may be places, especially in very hilly country, that a small hound is best. In this section, give me a good, medium large dog, say from 22 to 24 inches at shoulder and built in proportion with from 16 to 18 inches earage. Color is a matter of taste. I believe that our English cousins breed them so straight that the spots and marks are stamped on all alike. I have heard it said so much that a stranger could hardly see any difference in a pack and when the American breeder gets to giving so much attention to their breeding, then we will soon have a true type of hound.

Then I will say courage, driving with courage goes largely, speed and voice, good sound chest and body, good wide head and long muzzle, good bone and heavy forearm, good long back, good sound feet, well padded, with black upper mouth, a hazel eye, a strong loin and not too much flank. Regardless of color you have my ideal fox hound.

CHAPTER XV.

PECULIARITIES OF DOGS AND PRACTICAL HINTS.

NEVER purchase a dog from an unknown party unless the said party can supply good references and testimonials regarding the square dealing and the merits of his strain of dogs. If a man cannot give you this, wait until you find one who can.

Some people are inclined to believe that a big dog cannot compete with a smaller one. Most of them have to come to this conclusion because they have seen some big sloppy and lazy hound, but take a big, well built, lively, fleet and nervous hound, and full of grit and he will hold his own and more. It is just like trying to make a pony cover the same ground as a roadster, declares a lover of hounds.

A pup of most any large breed of dogs will make a good watch dog if properly brought up. If fondled and played with while young by everybody that happened to come to the house, then the dog will be playful and friendly with people always later on. If to be made cross and shun strangers, the pup should be reared in a lot with high board fence to prevent him seeing what goes on outside. The owner, in disguise, or better still some other person, should now and then pound against the fence, look over the top so the dog gets a glimpse at supposed intruders; partly open the gate and peek in, let the dog make a rush towards him but slam gate shut before quite coming up, etc. Such practice will make any dog watchful and cross towards all strangers, and will never make friends with any but his master. For an imposing, powerful and the best of watch dogs get a Mastiff or a Great Dane.

It is not wise to expect too much of a new dog. Some of them will fret and worry after their friends and home for a long time, will hardly eat or drink, and it takes the best of care and attention to bring good results. Eventually they will become acquainted and regain their old form, if properly encouraged.

I never pet my dogs while hunting except after killing game which in my opinion is pretty good policy as a dog like a man likes to have credit for what he had done. Remember also, though contrary to the old fashioned theory that it is just as unreasonable to ask a dog to hunt without food as it would be to hitch up a horse and drive him all day without either hay or grain, there has been many a good dog called a "quitter" simply because he was weak from the

PECULIARITIES OF DOGS, ETC.

lack of food. As for a quitter, in my opinion a vast majority of them have never commenced, not because they had a "yellow streak," as most hunters say, but because like the Irishman's pig, they have too many streaks of lean. As your dog is a better friend to you than most people of the J. Sneakum caliber, why not treat him right?

In some journals there is considerable criticism and complaints, and sometimes one feels like steering shy of many advertisements of fox hounds. One publication invites all persons to inform its editor where any dog has been misrepresented and sold through its columns. No doubt in many instances it may be the fault of the purchaser handling a strange dog. I purchased a dog that followed at my heels for several trips and would not leave me until one day he put his nose in a fresh trail. The other dog was out of hearing when he went out in a good race, tongueing in good shape, and was a No. 1 fox hound.

When a sportsman wishes to purchase a strange hound if he desires to get a good one he must pay the price and the way for him to not be fooled is to deposit his money at the express office and then have the dog sent on trial and if not satisfactory, he returns the dog and pays the express charges one way. This is the only safe way to get a good dog, as a man that will accept these conditions will most certainly send you the right stuff at once and not a "cull", that he has scraped somewhere for $5.00 and sells you from $15 to $30.

It's detrimental to allow a bird dog to roam and go self-hunting. Not being restricted he gets in all sorts of mischief. Keeping at home is the only remedy. To give ample exercise arrange a trolley in the yard by driving two stakes into ground without projecting; fasten a strong wire to top of posts and on this slip a ring to slide on; to this snap the chain and the dog can run up and down the full length of wire. Within a few days he will learn the extent of run and chase up and down the full length for hours at a time, then be content and restful.

By nature dogs are cleanly and will not soil their bed or kennel if to be avoided. Being shut up in a small place may cause them to be uncleanly and soil the floor, making it disagreeable, as by rolling in play all the dogs will constantly present soiled appearance. However, even in a small kennel this can be regulated as follows: Thoroughly clean out the place and scrub; in one corner bore some holes into floor and spread sawdust over this part only; litter the rest of space with clean straw and besprinkle this with some strong disinfectant. Turn in the dogs. At once one or more will go to sawdust portion, — this done the ice is broken and henceforth all the dogs will use this part only as retiring place, leaving the remainder perfectly clean.

Teach your hound not to be afraid of water, and to circle the tree and to keep an eye on the coon and to bark treed, but never allow him to get whipped by any coon at first as this will discourage him. Not only this, but the coon may blind him should he strike him in the eye. It is better always to hold or tie the dog before shooting the coon, and when he drops to make sure that he cannot fight much more before allowing the dog near him.

CHAPTER XVI.

AILMENTS OF THE DOG.

DOGS as well as people sometimes fall ill. Proper care and sanitary lodgings will reduce the danger, but sickness will occasionally occur, no matter how great the precautions.

Dog owners should therefore acquaint themselves with the commoner forms of ailment to which dogs are subject and thus be in a position to quickly administer such relief as is possible, thereby frequently stopping a sick spell promptly that might otherwise result seriously if not fatally.

The dog is very similar to man in his ailments as well as in his susceptibility to drugs. As a general thing medicine that is good for a human being is good for a dog under similar circumstances. "While no definite rule can be laid down" says an eminent authority, "it may be said that a dose suitable for an adult person is correct for the largest dogs, such as St. Bernards; for dogs from forty to fifty pounds the dose should correspond with that given to a child twelve to fourteen years of age, and so on down."

AILMENTS OF THE DOG. 147

Few veterinarians make a study of the dog, and they rarely are of any use when called. However, those who have made a special study may be consulted with advantage and saving.

We have not the space here to go into an exhaustive recitation of dog diseases, symptoms, treatment and remedies. If you are at a loss concerning your dog, write to one of the Dog Doctors, whose advertisements appear in sporting magazines, and he can no doubt diagnose the case and forward the medicine you require at a minimum cost. In nearly all cases he will forward you a free booklet describing the prevalent diseases and his remedies applicable to same.

The following from the pen of H. Clay Glover, V. S., will no doubt give many readers some light on one of the common afflictions that prove sc troublesome.

INDIGESTION IN DOGS.

Eczema is a frequent symptom, and let me state right here that I find more cases of eczematous eruptions arising from a disordered condition of the digestion than any other cause. Doubtless many who will read this will recognize the fact that at some time some certain dog has had some obstinate skin trouble, all kinds of which are by the layman diagnosed as "mange", and that, after trying various mange cures to which the trouble has not yielded, the blood has been treated with no better results.

To any one who have, or may have in the future, indigestion cases, let me advise the following treatment, viz.: Feed rather sparingly three times a day on raw or scraped beef, this being the most readily accepted and most easily digested of all foods when the digestion is disordered, allowing no other diet, and giving immediately after each meal one of the digestive pills. Add to the drinking water lime water in the proportion of one to thirty.

By following this treatment as laid down, many cases of eczema will disappear. Some probably, may be accelerated by the use of a skin lotion in conjunction. Eczema in these cases is merely a symptom appearing in evidence of disordered digestion. Indigestion may be considered as a mild form of gastritis, which if not corrected, will be followed by true gastritis, the stomach then being in such condition that nothing is retained, even water being returned immediately after drinking. This will be accompanied by fever, colic, emaciation and only too often followed by death.

DISTEMPER.

We quote further from Dr. Glover's booklet,

AILMENTS OF THE DOG. 149

some practical information on another of the more common dog ailments:

The term distemper is particularly applied to animals of the brute creation; to the dog when afflicted with that disease somewhat resembling typhus fever in the human race. We have now become quite familiar with the nature of the disease and the remedies indicated; consequently the loss by death is comparatively small when proper treatment and attention are employed. In early days, those dogs that were fortunate enough to survive this disease did so merely through strength of constitution and not from the assistance of any remedial agent, as utter ignorance of the subject then prevailed. The disease doubtless then appeared in a much milder form than that with which our present highly bred animals are afflicted.

Owing to more or less inbreeding that has been indulged in to intensify certain forms and characteristics in dogs of most all breeds, constitution has to some extent been sacrificed. Animals bred in this way are in consequence less able to resist or combat disease than those with less pretentious claims to family distinction.

CAUSES — Bad sanitary conditions, crowded or poorly drained kennels, exposure to dampness, insufficient or over feeding, improper diet, lack of fresh air and exercise, all conduce to the development of distemper. It is contagious, infectious, and will frequently appear spontaneously without any apparent cause in certain localities, assuming an epidemic form. Age is no exemption from distemper, though it more frequently attacks young animals than adults. Very few dogs pass through life without having it at some period.

SYMPTOMS — In early stages, dullness, loss of appetite, sneezing, chills, fever, undue moisture of the nose, congestion of the eyes, nausea, a gagging cough accompanied by the act of vomition, though rarely anything is voided (if anything, it will be a little mucous), thirst, a desire to lie in a warm place, and rapid emaciation. This is quickly followed by mucopurulent discharge from the eyes and nose; later, perhaps, ulceration of either eyes or eyelids. Labored respiration, constipation or obstinate diarrhoea, usually the latter, which frequently runs into inflammation of the bowels.

In some cases many of the above symptoms will be absent, the bowels being the first parts attacked. The following, which sometimes, but not necessarily, occur with distemper, I classify as complications, viz.: Fits, Chorea, Paralysis, Pneumonia or Bronco-Pneumonia, Jaundice, and Inflammation of the Bowels, and will require

AILMENTS OF THE DOG. 151

treatment independent of any one remedy that may be given.

TREATMENT — The animal should be placed in warm, dry quarters, and hygienic conditions strictly observed. With puppies, at the start give vermifuge, as nearly all have worms which add greatly to the irritation of stomach, bowels and nervous system.

The bedding should be changed daily and the apartment disinfected twice a week.

Feed frequently on easily digested, nutritious diet, such as beef tea or mutton broth, thickened with rice. Let all food be slightly cool, and keep fresh cold water at all times within reach of the animal. If constipation be present give warm water and glycerine enemas, and an occasional dose of castor oil if necessary. Should the bowels become too much relaxed with any tendency to inflammation, feed entirely upon food, such as arrowroot, farina or corn starch with well boiled milk, as even beef tea is somewhat of an irritation to the stomach and bowels.

In the treatment of distemper, one great object is to keep up the general strength, so in case of extreme debility a little whisky in milk or milk punches may be allowed.

If your efforts are not successful and you are in danger of losing one or more good dogs, write a specialist. It would require fifty pages of this book to go into the subject fully.

RHEUMATISM.

Acute rheumatism in the dog is similar to that in the human body, effecting the joints. Muscular rheumatism settles in the muscles. If given early 5 to 15 grains, twice a day, of salicate of sodium is a most excellent preventative measure. A severe case demands more elaborate care.

RICKETS.

Those accustomed to dogs have seen cases of rickets. It is a constitutional or inherited affliction, and attacks puppies most frequently. Nothing can be done save kill the sufferer if the attack is severe, or build up the health generally, toward outgrowing the trouble, if mild.

These are only a few of the ailments the faithful dog is heir to; yet in a general way, a healthy dog is no more subject to disease than a healthy person, and in many cases the old family watch dog will pass a long and useful life with no more serious trouble than he can readily cope with, with the assistance of nature.

We add some practical advice from Mr. Amer Braley of Dade Co., Florida, as to what will cure canker in the ears of dogs, a prevalent and aggravating trouble: Will say I have cured cases of it of long standing by working boracic acid well into their ears, usually a few applications does the work.

There is a disease that kills more dogs in Florida than all the other causes put together. It is called sore mouth, black tongue, new disease and other names. I lost some fine hounds of this disease, usually dying from six to eight days from the time of showing disease. Symptoms of it are generally languor, dullness about the eyes, little or no appetite, sometimes feverish and a dryness about the mouth and at other times slobbers hang down from the mouth.

They seem anxious to drink water but are unable to swallow it. Their tongues seem to be somewhat paralyzed, they can hardly pick up anything. They usually want to roam around where they will not be molested. I will give a remedy that I have which has cured several cases of this disease with the only ones I ever knew to survive it. I will give it for it may be the means of saving the lives of some good dogs.

"A gelatin coated pill or capsule of quinine containing five grains twice a day for two days, then one each day for a week." Also swab out their mouth with the following: "Chlorate potassium half ounce, murvate tincture iron half ounce. Put into one pint of water and shake well. Tie rag or cotton to stick, letting it protrude over the end, and swab out the mouth two or three times a day."

You want to go right at once to giving the remedy for if the disease runs 36 hours I don't think there is any cure for it. The size doses mentioned here are for good-sized dogs as grown hounds. Smaller ones and pups reduce accordingly.

There is another disease that dogs are sometimes taken with in this country. Some say it is caused by ticks. It is called "staggers" as the dog that is affected with it staggers as he walks. It seems as though they can't manage their hind parts. Sometimes they break down and have to drag their hind parts (sled fashion.)

A remedy that I have never known to fail yet for that is: Lard and spirits of turpentine about equal parts mixed and bathe in well across the kidneys and also across the back of head where it joins to neck. Usually two or three applications makes a cure.

PART III.

DOG LORE.

Two Good Dogs and 14 Coon they Helped Dispatch.

CHAPTER XVII.

STILL TRAILERS VS. TONGUERS. MUSIC.

PERHAPS no more mooted question enters in for so widely separated opinion as the comparative superiority of the Still Trailing dog and the Tonguers.

The still or mute trailer is the deer, rabbit or night dog which does not give tongue on the trail. He keeps his silence, until his game is treed or in sight and about to tree.

The tonguer gives forth a joyous and lusty cry as soon as he makes a strike, and continues to do so until the chase terminates. When treed he changes his bark, so that usually the hunter can distinguish between the signals.

We shall withhold personal opinion as to the preferable style, and present the arguments of a number of adherents on both sides of the question, allowing the reader to come to his own conclusion.

A West Virginia 'coon expert says, in favor of the tonguer: I have had several good 'coon dogs, both tonguers and silent trailers. This is a hilly, brushy country, with lots of deep hollows. The best 'coon dog I ever had was a three-fourths fox hound, one-fourth bull dog. He was very fast with a good nose and a wide hunter. He never struck a cold trail and went straight ahead all the time. He has started a 'coon half a mile away from me and would go right out of hearing of me, and I would follow the way I would judge the 'coon to travel and would be hours finding him barking treed. If he had been a mute trailer I would have left him in the woods without the slightest idea where he was and that is no fun when you have gone three or four miles walk from home to get a 'coon chase.

Another brother puts it this way: Some hunters prefer a still trailer on a cold trail. I have handled both kinds but it is an advantage to the hunter in keeping in touch with his hound if the hound will "wind his horn" occasionally on a cold trail for very often a wide hound will travel a couple of miles on a cold trail before starting the game. In windy weather, the hunters might be at a loss to know in which direction his dog was working, if he did not hear him. I like a dog with a loud, clear voice and one that keeps the music going steady once the game is afoot."

Still another gives voice to his sentiment thus: I want a good tonguer, one that will give me no trouble in keeping the direction they are going. One that is a courser, that is, that never foots around trying to find every track a 'coon makes, but keeps on finding ahead anywhere from a hundred yards to a quarter of a mile. That kind of a dog keeps you awake when cold trailing, and is apt to warm up at any time.

A Western tonguer adherent says: For 'coon I like the cold trailer that lets you know where he is going, and don't believe they will hole any sooner for him than a still trailer, and I never saw a full blooded hound still track. My hounds give a long whoop every few rods on cold trail, and will "back brush" a 'coon or wolf that is many hours old but will find him, and you can follow up so as to keep in hearing. My dogs are quite fast but I do not go back on a moderately slow dog to shoot after. I think they circle better.

From Indian Territory comes this addition to the testimony: The thoroughbred hound for 'coon is my view after 40 years' experience. A good many are giving their idea as to which is best, the still trailer or the dog that gives tongue. I have never known a thoroughbred hound fail to give tongue on trail. The thoroughbred has the greatest powers of scent and this is very important as you do not have to travel so much ground to find a trail that he can run. What we want when we go after 'coon is to start and catch all we can. If we cannot start one we cannot catch him, sure. I have followed behind over the same ground with my hound that another party had been over with their still trailers and caught more 'coon than they.

And again if you are out on a windy night and your still trailer gets a 'coon treed to the windward of you, you might as well go home as there will be no more fun for you if he is a good tree dog.

Now just one thing more in regard to still trailers catching 'coon on the ground. That has not been my experience, for you all know when you go a rabbit hunting with a still trailer, how soon the rabbit will hole. He has no warning where the dog is, so in trailing 'coon, the 'coon will wait and listen to the hound and if he is a fast runner, Mr. 'Coon has waited too long. He must make for the nearest tree or get caught. With the still trailer, the 'coon hears the leaves and brush snapping and without any more warning makes for his home tree.

Hundreds of hunters take this view, that is, favor the dog which barks from the time he takes up the trail. The principal advantage as has been pointed out, is that the hound and hunter may thus keep in closer touch, and that the hunter is treated to "music," so sweet to the ear of the average enthusiast.

STILL TRAILERS VS. TONGUERS. MUSIC.

Another considerable following, however, at once take issue and present an array of argument in favor of the dog which keeps his silence

Let us first consider the views of a conservative Pennsylvania brother, in favor of the still trailer: I see a good many 'coon hunters disagree on 'coon dogs, still trailers vs. tongueing dogs. Now in my experience, I have used nearly all kinds of 'coon dogs, some good ones and some not so good. I think the difference is in the kind of country to be hunted, for hunting in a very rough country that is cut up by long hollows and large tracts of timber I prefer a tongueing dog.

For hunting in this locality where it is all cut up into small fields with principally all rail fences and timber in small blocks, mostly cut over by lumbermen and nothing left but hollow trees and brush, I prefer a still trailer by long odds, as the noisy dog gives the 'coon warning as soon as he strikes the trail, then Mr. 'Coon takes to the rail fence or a jungle of briers and old tree tops and begins to get busy and is soon in one of those hollow trees, where he is perfectly safe as far as I am concerned, for I never cut down any den trees.

The still trailer does his work quietly and is right on to the 'coon before it is aware that the dog is after it. So Mr. 'Coon is obliged to climb whatever kind of a tree there is handy and very often is taken on the ground.

From a Central States hunter's letter: I used to be a dear lover of a dog that would bark on trail and raise some of them, but now my choice is a still trailer, as a quiet trailer suits this locality best on account of the thickly populated country and the great amount of stock raised, and a great many farmers claim the constant barking of dogs frightens their sheep. For that reason fox chasing is fast losing its interest and foxes are becoming quite a nuisance in the destruction of quail, pheasant, rabbit and such like game.

A brother of conviction on this question writes: It takes patience, perseverance and skill to properly train a hound for 'coon. First, the dog must be silent until he finds the hot scent, so as not to give Mr. 'Coon time to commence his sunny ways, as the 'coon has a good knowledge box and lots of strings to his bow which he uses to evade Mr. Hound. He will swim down and sometimes up stream and often crosses them. Will never miss a hollow log and comes out at the other end, and will climb leaning trees and leap from them to others and may return to the stream for a good long swim before he will make quietly for his den. This is what an old 'coon will often do with a noisy dog, but with a swift and silent one he will have to climb at once and stay there.

Another telling stroke for silence: Regarding silent trailers: By silent trailer I mean a dog that will not tongue the very instant he finds an old trail when there is yet some scent, but that will work it quietly until he starts the game. I have often seen hounds roar on an old scent as well as on a new one. These dogs have generally a special gait, which they keep steady whether the trail is cold or hot, and give the full cry the whole time, and also often come to a full stop to blast away a few louder roars. These dogs dwell too long on the scent for me. My strain of dogs will open only when they are on a hot scent; if cold, they will cover the ground silently and fast.

A swift dog cannot keep up the full cry, but will give a roar now and then and not bark often as it takes a lot of wind to roar. Therefore, a dog cannot be a flyer and a roarer in the meantime, and a deer, fox, lynx or 'coon, chased by a fleet and silent dog as above mentioned, will have to point at once for safety, and will have no spare time for tricks. The lynx or 'coon will have to climb in a hurry the first tree he finds, while with a noisy dog Mr. 'Coon will commence with his tricks as soon as he will hear the music, and I maintain and stand ready to prove that a silent trailer as I have described will water more deer in five hours in this country than a noisy one will in five days.

THE MUSIC OF THE HOUND.

The term "music" as applied to the barking

"He Was Here a Moment Ago!"

of trailing hunting dogs, is to the uninitiated a gross misnomer.

"Isn't that music grand!" exclaimed an enthusiast afield.

"I can hear no music for the noise those dogs are making," replied the other. And so it goes.

The hound is the master orator, with a command of language that varies from uncertainty, joy, anxiety, conviction, eagerness with great clearness and truth. His shades of meaning are accurately intonated and perfectly comprehendible to the well versed hunter.

The hound is looked upon with disdain by people who know not his capabilities, and is considered in the nature of the dunce of the tribe. Well do the well informed know that he is the most delicately strung and the most highly emotional type we have.

Every note that he utters is an expression of emotion. Because emotion is more susceptible to music than any other agency, his code of expression is likened unto notes of music, and with more fidelity than some instrumental sound producers committed in the name of music.

A student of this pure and undefiled language says: "Each note represents a particular feeling, and the whole harmoniously blended, tells a simple story in a pleasing way."

Now the hound takes up the cold trail. He signals his master — there are notes of expectancy and hope in the tone. As the scent grows warmer, his tone of hope rises. He makes a loss. Could anything express regret and chagrin any more plainly than his doleful cry? Back on the trail. Then joy again. Then comes the excited, imperative, anxious yet joyous fortissimo scale running when the quarry trees.

"Here He Is!"

He who has not been schooled in classical music sits bored and alone at the production of an opera, or yawns and wishes he were at home in bed, as the vigorous long haired performer spells out his emotions on the piano key board. So it is that one with no ear for music of the hound is disgusted thruout the sally to the woods at night, or the fields by day. He can dwell upon nothing save the scratches, falls and efforts required, all of which another forgets in fixing his attention on the action and music of the chase.

Some hounds are better singers than others, just as is the case with people. Also he must be trained to perform pleasingly and truly. If he is well trained and is certain in his movements it will be reflected in his music. If he is faulty in foot and head work he will also betray these faults in his voice. Anxious to cover his own shortcomings, he takes to guessing and guesses wrong. He becomes a liar, and his singing is like unto the fellow with a cracked voice who insists on singing in the church choir, thereby annoying everybody.

An experienced hunter can tell by the song of a hound how capable he is, even if there were not many other ways of fixing values.

Bring up a hound under proper training methods, and he is almost certain to prove a rare musician.

If you are not versed in music of this kind, you are unfortunate, and should join the fox or 'coon hunters and take a course of lessons. It is well worth while.

CHAPTER XVIII.

THE DOG ON THE TRAP LINE

SOME trappers will take issue in regard to the advantages and disadvantages of the dog on the trap line.

The subject holds sufficient interest, however, to warrant a chapter, and if some lonesome trappers benefit thereby, our effort shall stand justified.

Now, we will say first that there is as much or more difference in the man who handles the dog as there is in the different breeds of dogs. We have heard men say that they wanted no dog on the trap line with them, and that they didn't believe that any one who did want a dog on the trap line knew but very little about trapping at the best.

Now those are the views and ideas of some trappers, while my experience has led me to see it otherwise. One who is so constituted that they must give a dog the growl or perhaps a kick every time they come in reach, will undoubtedly find a dog of but little use on the trap line. We have known some dogs to refuse to eat, and would lay out where they could watch in

THE DOG ON THE TRAP LINE.

the direction in which their master had gone and piteously howl for hours, waiting the return of the master and friend. I have seen other dogs that would take for the barn or any other place to get out of the way at the first sight or sound of their master. This man's dog is usually more attached to a stranger than to his master. The man who cannot treat his dog as a friend and companion will have good cause to say that a dog is a nuisance on the trap line.

I have seen men training dogs for bird hunting, who would treat the dog most cruelly and claim that a dog could not be trained to work a bird succesfully under any other treatment. Though I have seen others train the same breed of dogs to work a bird to perfection and that their most harsh treatment would be a tap or two with a little switch. I will say that one who cannot understand the wag of a dog's tail, the wistful gaze of the eye, the quick lifting of the ears, the cautious raising of a foot, and above all, treat his dog as a friend, need expect his dog to be but little else than a nuisance on the trap line.

Several years ago I had a partner who had a dog, part stag hound and the other part just dog, I think. One day he (my partner) asked if I would object to his bringing the dog to camp, saying that his wife was going on a visit and he had no place to leave the dog. I told him that if he had a good dog I would be glad to have him in camp. In a day or two pard went home and brought in the dog. Well, when he came the dog was following along behind his master with tail and ears drooping, and looking as though he never heard a kind word in his life. I asked if the animal was any good and he replied that he did not know how good he was. I asked the name of the dog. He said, "Oh, I call him Pont." I spoke to the dog, calling him by name. He looked at me wistfully, wagging his tail. The look that dog gave me said to me as plainly as words that this was the first kind word he had ever heard.

We went inside and the dog started to follow, when his master in a harsh voice said, "get out of here." I said, "where do you expect the dog to go?" I then took an old coat that was in the camp, placed it in the corner and called gently to Pont, patted the coat and told him to lay down on the coat, which he did. I patted him saying that is a good place for Pont, and I can see that wistful gaze the dog gave me, now. After we had our supper I asked my partner if he wasn't going to fix Pont some supper. "Oh, after a while I will see if I can't find something for him." I took a biscuit from the table, spread some butter on it, called the dog to me, broke

THE DOG ON THE TRAP LINE. 171

the biscuit in pieces, and gave it to the dog from my hand; then I found an old basin that chanced to be about the camp and fixed the dog a good supper.

After the dog had finished his supper I went to the coat in the corner, spoke gently to Pont, patted the coat, and told him to lay down on the coat. That was the end of that, Pont knew his place and took it without any further rouble.

The next morning when we were about ready to start out on the trap line I asked Pard what he intended to do with Pont. He said that he would tie him to a tree that stood against the shanty close to the door. We were going to take different lines of traps. I said, "What is the harm of Pont's going with me?" "All right, if you want him, I don't want any dog with me." I said, "Am, (that was Pard's given name, for short) I don't believe the dog wants to go with you any more than you want him to. Am's reply was that he guessed he would go all right if he wanted him. I said, Am, just for shucks, say nothing to the dog and see which one he will follow. So we stepped outside the shack and the dog stood close to me.

I said, "Go on Am, and we will see who the dog will follow." He started off and the dog only looked at him. Am stopped and told the dog to come on. The dog got around behind me.

Am said, "If I wanted you to come, you would come or I would break your neck." I said, "No, Am, you won't break Pont's neck while I am around; it would not look nice."

I started on my way, Pont following after I had gone a little ways. I spoke to Pont, patting him on the head and told him what a good dog he was. He jumped about and showed more ways than one how pleased he was, and from that day until we broke camp, Pont stayed with me. He showed plainly the disgust he had for his master.

It so happened that the first trap I came to was a trap set in a spring run, and it had a 'coon in it. I allowed Pont to help kill the 'coon, and after the 'coon was dead, I patted Pont and told him what great things he had done in capturing the 'coon. Pont showed what pride he took in the hunt, so much so that he did not like to have Am go near the pelt. I saw from the very first day out that all that Pont needed was kind treatment and proper training to make a good help on the trap line.

I was careful to let him know what I was doing when setting a trap, and when he would go to smell at the bait after a trap had been set, I would speak to him in a firm voice and let him know that I did not approve of what he was doing. When making blind sets, I took the same pains to show and give him to understand what I was doing. I would sometimes, after giving him fair warning, let him put his foot into a trap. I would scold him in a moderate manner and release him. Then all the time I was resetting the trap I would talk trap to him, and by action and word teach him the nature of the trap. Mr. Trapper, please do not persuade yourself to believe that the intelligent dog cannot understand if you go about it right.

In two weeks Pont had advanced so far in his training that I no longer had to pay any attention to him on account of the traps. The third day Pont was with me he found a 'coon that had escaped with a trap nearly two weeks before. My route called me up a little draw from the main stream. I had not gone far up this when Pont took the trail of some animal and began working it up the side of the hill. I stood and watched him until the trail took him to an old log, when Pont began to sniff at a hole in the log. He soon raised his head and gave a long howl, as much as to say he is here and I want help. After running a stick in the hole I soon discovered that the log was hollow. I took my belt axe and pounded along on the log until I thought I was at the right point and then chopped a hole in the log, and as good luck would have it, I made the opening right on to the 'coon, and almost the first thing I saw on looking into the log was the trap. Pont soon had the 'coon out, and when I saw it was the 'coon that had escaped with our trap, I gave Pont praise for what he had done, petting him and telling him of his good deed, and he seemed to understand it all.

Not long after this Am came into camp at night and reported that a fox had broken the chain on a certain trap and gone off with the trap, saying that he would take Pont in the morning and see if he could find the fox. In the morning when we were ready to go Am tried to have Pont follow him, but it was no go, Pont would not go with him. Then Am put a rope on to him and tried to lead him, but Pont would sulk and would not be led. Then Am lost his temper and wanted to break Pont's neck again. I said that I did not like to have Pont abused and that I would go along with him. When we came to the place where the fox had escaped with the trap Am at once began to slap his hands and hiss Pont on. Pont only crouched behind me for protection. I persuaded Am to go on down the run and look at the traps down that way while I and Pont would look after the escaped fox.

As soon as Am was gone I began to look about where the fox had been caught and search

THE DOG ON THE TRAP LINE. 175

for his trail, and soon Pont began to wag his tail. I merely worked Pont's way and said, "Has he gone that way?" Pont gave me to understand that the fox had gone that way and that he knew what was wanted. The trail soon left the main hollow and took up a little draft. A little way up this we found where the fox had been fast in some bushes but had freed himself and left and gone up the hillside. Pont soon began to get uneasy, and when I said hunt him out Pont, away he went and in a few minutes I heard Pont give a long howl and I knew that he had holed his game. When I came up to Pont he was working in a hole in some shell rocks. I pulled away some loose rocks and could see the fox, and we soon had him out, and Pont seemed more pleased over the hunt than I was. There was scarcely a week that Pont did not help us out on the trap line.

Not unfrequently did Pont show me a 'coon den. I had some difficulty in teaching Pont to let the porcupines alone, but after a time he learned that they were not the kind of game that he wanted, and he paid no more attention to them.

I have had many different dogs on the trap line with me, and I can say to any one who can understand dog's language, has a liking for a dog and has a reasonable amount of patience and is willing to use it, will find a well trained dog of much benefit on the trap line, and often a more genial companion than some partners one may fall in with. But if one is so constituted that he must give his dog a growl or a kick every time he comes in reach, and perhaps only give his dog half enough to eat and cannot treat a dog as a friend, then I say, leave the dog off the trap line.

A Group of Typical Sledge Dogs.

CHAPTER XIX.

SLEDGE DOGS OF THE NORTH

NOT a hunting dog in a strict sense of the word, yet most important in that connection, is the sledge dog, in transportation of hunters and their outfits to and from the hunting and trapping scenes.

Following is a first hand, specially written article by Colonel F. H. Buzzacott, the intrepid Arctic explorer. That he writes from experience is evident, which necessarily adds interest and value to his highly interesting contribution.

What the Indian pony is to the plain Indian, the Pack Horse or Mule is to the White Settler, Hunter or Trapper, the Sledge Dog or Reindeer is to natives of the distant and Far North. An old saying among frontiersmen is that a white man will abandon a horse as broken down and utterly unable to go when a Mexican will take that same horse and make him go a hundred miles further, while an Indian after all of this will mount and ride him for a week still.

With all Indians, natives of the north or Esquimaux, knives are luxuries, ponies and dogs, necessities. Yet, for all that, they are never stabled, curried, washed, blanketed, shod, seldom protected or even fed. When the icy cold wintry blasts sweep the drifting snows over plain and valley and buries under his white mantle his food he either digs for it, finds and eats what he can, or starves.

In my plains experience with the Indians or in the Polar Regions with the natives of the north or Esquimaux, I have observed that the love of an Indian for his ponies, an Esquimaux for his dogs or Laplander for his reindeer consists in seeing how much he really can get out of them with the least trouble or effort to him.

I have seen the Indians or natives of the northwest and the Esquimaux of Hudson's and Baffin's Bay, Greenland, etc., drive half starved dogs to the sledge until they fell or froze, only to be eaten by their masters or mates, whom for a lifetime they had pulled with or served faithfully. Necessity recognizes no law—man is but an animal himself — and in the struggle for life or gain it is everywhere but the "Survival of the Fittest" or strongest and passing of the weak, be it white man or Indian.

The best of the 'Sledge Dogs of the North" are to be found in Greenland or Siberia, "Samoyed" dogs or its Esquimaux cousin, the "Immit Dog", used by explorers and Esquimaux generally. Those with short, thick hair, medium build, size and full breed are considered the best for all around work. They will exist and work well on one pound of food per day, or a big feast once a week. Their food consists mostly of dried and fresh fish, carrion or fresh, or, if with explorers, dog biscuit added.

They closely resemble a wolf and howl like one. Are of various colors and sizes, iron grey predominating. They average about two feet four inches in height by three feet six inches in length, of unusually light weight for their size, owing to the bristle out appearance of their hair which adds to their real size. As a rule females are killed at birth, except those few to suffice for breeding. Commence training at six months to a year old and when two or three years old and seasoned to work are considered prime and preferable for long heavy distant sledging and hunting.

The best trained of the team (eight, twelve or more in number) is selected as a leader. They are guided by voice and whip, a loud "Brr-Brr" taking the place of our "Gee" in starting and the word "Sass-Sass" used as "Whoa." "Hi" and "He" for right and left, "Ho" to correct, or speed, as they are trained, of course. A good leader possesses the quality of rarely failing to lead one safely over any route once traveled by them, bringing you safely to the place even if buried under the snow.

They eat each other's flesh wolf-like with gusto and will tear their fellows to pieces in fight or injury, unless beaten, torn apart or separated by a man of whom they are afraid. They hate water in winter as much as they love it in summer when they frequent the salmon streams and support themselves by fishing, pounce upon nearing fish of any size that approach them, much as does the bear, two of them even tackling an immensely big fish and fighting to secure and bring it to shore. As bear, muskox, or reindeer, dogs, a pack of them will invariably round up, hold or drive anything sighted within reasonable distance so long as the hunters will follow on, needing but little urging, as they realize the prospect of a "good big feast," hence get busy to the end; younger dogs often paying the penalty with their lives but seldom older ones.

As a rule, rawhide or seal harness is used in the far north, Alaska and Greenland and by the Esquimaux but with the explorers these consist mostly of canvas collar like attachments made of fourfold strips, two of which pass or slip over the critter's back, the other two between the forelegs, the whole united to a trace and this in turn fastened by a toggle, hook or ring to the sledge or drag rope. The dogs are hitched to this, either side of the drag, or alternately single or double, distant a few feet from each other. The guiding dog or leader is ahead leading while the others follow. Where canvas harness or steel wire rope is used on the drag by "Expeditions" it is because it lessens the chances of the harness being stolen, chewed or eaten, when rations become scarce.

In heavy traveling they are used and hitched double for fast travel, alternate and single as exigencies require and will travel from 10 to 50 miles a day according to conditions of road, load, snow, ice, etc. When hitched or prior to it, they are usually lightly fed so as to bring them to reach their destination and "Tether," loafers soon learn that they must earn their food. At times when worked hard, they get off feed, so to speak, sulk and refuse to come up to a drag. In which case the remaining dogs must do the work and rarely do they fail to whine, show their contempt for such action and punish "His Nibs" at the first chance later on, even pining to get at him, sled and all, as they observe him following behind alone.

On hard pulls, or uneven drags, they play out easily, act mulish, refusing to budge until the sled is started or at variance with each other. Otherwise, the start is a steady pull until well under way. A good team double will pull easily

SLEDGE DOGS OF THE NORTH. 183

a load of 1,000 pounds or more- single about one-half, depending largely on condition of themselves and the road they travel. The Esquimaux seldom spares them or the whip, "Brring" them on and "Hi-ying" if needs be.

About eight hours' work constitutes a day's travel or they go until played out, the latter case most likely. When traveling they are fairly obedient and preserve a steady equal pulling that occasionally is relieved by a jerky, gallop-like pace. Well trained dogs preserve their pace and tug on the harness for hours at a time. Usually they stop every hour or so for breathing spells as the atmosphere in those regions winds them easily. If traveling fast on ice and one falls or slips, he is dragged along, half strangled, until he regains his feet, place and position in line again, or, becoming tangled he is loosened up. By this time he has been snapped a few times by the dogs about him as if to punish him for his carelessness.

Ordinarily, the leader responds promptly to the driver's voice, guiding, turning, halting or increasing speed at the given command. When, however, they scent game, they become difficult to manage, requiring utmost application of the whip to keep the trail or direction and this invariably ends in confusion, hopeless tangle and upset sledge.

Handling, feeding, training calls for more judgment and patience than skill, driving especially. They refuse to cross apparently weak yet tested ice, pressure ridges, ice or snow cracks and mulelike, will make a plunging jump over a depression (when in trace) which ordinarily

Sledge Dog.—Photo From Life.

would not call for a leap at all. They require watchfulness on the part of the driver over cross country or when not following the trail, lest they sheer off from a given direction or straight line.

When following the trail much confidence is vested in the leader and should perchance it strike a blind or cross trail, it will howl to attract the attention of the driver and by these means verify directions, as if to ask if it is leading right. In case it loses the track it will slow up, whine, run up or "criss-cross its tracks, sniffing and smelling in an anxious, expectant way, until it finds or is led correct, when it howls with delight and pulls off "like blazes" again.

They have strange likes and dislikes. As entire pack will punish one who incurs the displeasure at times to an extent of crippling or killing each other. If a strange dog comes amongst them he is pretty sure to get "mauled" or his scraping abilities put to test, which usually ends in a free-for-all fight, catch as catch can rules predominating.

When in harness training a young dog gets punished frequently by its mates for any awkwardness it shows. Old dogs especially show contempt for a new or strange dog which takes its mate's place, be it pup or otherwise, and will often sulk if their place is changed. Each seems to think his place is best, the leader especially being particularly proud of his honored position in "Dogdom." As a rule, existing difficulties or arguments in harness are stored up until that day's march is over, because of fear of punishment from the driver, but as soon as turned loose, they settle the difficulty of the day by another scrap, in which often one bunch will participate in, 'take sides," and chew up each other, until all pitch in, aiming to settle things somehow. If too tired, they await the morrow. As a rule, the best sledge dogs are the poorest scrappers (so we have to be partial at times) especially to the leader who is usually the most intelligent; hence favored.

In a pinch, when game and rations are scarce, they make good eating, of course, being sacrificed. At these times, their peculiar savage nature asserts itself, when you kill one for food, by signs of joy, rather than fear for they seem to be devoid of sympathy or unaffected by the scene. Their flesh is pale, tender and tasteless much like rabbit, bloodless and poor, and they will eat anything from a tin can label to Kipling's "Rag, Bone or Hank of Hair." When meat is plenty, they take on flesh and fatten quickly but seldom does this happen as the Esquimaux says, "Him no good, lazy, much fat."

Wolf-like, stolen food tastes better and one will leave his own ration to steal a fellow's equal share and risking by his greediness both, as it is stolen in turn by another. Their thieving propensities are great, a tin can of meat, skin boots, oil lamp, old soup kettle, or their own harness if sealskin or rawhide.

Tied, penned up or left harnessed **any**

length of time, they assert their belief in "Liberty and Equality" by chewing their way to freedom if it takes a week to do it. As a rule, the

Rough and Ready Sledge Dog.

dogs respect a female and will seldom molest her. These give birth to a litter of from 4 to 8 pups which are generally killed at birth, unless a scarcity of them, fat "puppy dog" being with the paunch of the reindeer considered a regular "Delmonico" dish. The average usefulness of their existence is about 6 to 8 years, the old dogs following the same road as fat puppies, after their usefulness has seen the limit. Fall bred dogs are best. Alaskan dogs are larger and heavier and the same rule applies to Labrador species, but as they are of mixed breed, lazier and require more food they are only used to advantage where they belong — at home.

As a rule, they exist, breed and sleep in the open, the soft side of a drifting snow bank being a luxury, especially if it drifts about them up to the muzzle, and it is only vacated when dangerous. They seek the warmest spots they can find, a rope coil, rag or paper, or even a tin can to lie on, in preference to ice or hard snow. Failing in this, they will dig a hole in the soft snow and bury themselves in this, lying one on top of the other in bitter weather. The best of Arctic or Polar dogs, while they withstand cold to surprising degree, nevertheless, suffer with the cold and danger of freezing, especially in winter time when food is scarce or frozen and snow serves to quench thirst, a wet foot or crippled limb being the first to suffer. In bitter weather I have seen them roll and run to maintain circulation. They huddle together, shivering, hold up their paws and whine pitifully and appealingly.

They receive a kind word by a show of teeth instead of a wag — indeed, are anything but friendly, except at "chuck" time and then limit it to the grub with a few exceptions, of course. Most of them, however, Indian-like, believe in the old maxim "Familiarity breeds contempt" and thus they treat kindness with suspicion and turn tail as if it preceded work or a licking and perhaps both.

If left alone any length of time, one will start up a coyote-like howl and all join in one after the other in the chorus that takes the appearance of a man with a "big stick" to quell. If left alone they will keep it up for hours, stopping as it commenced by degrees, apparently without reason. They are fed when circumstances permit and if permitted, will gorge themselves to the point of bursting, eating enough to last a week and camping alongside of it until even the bones are cleaned up and not enough left to feed a fly. Indian-like, however, they are always on hand for the next meal, hungry again. When traveling, they are fed a little daily, but when not, exist on wind, bones and kicks, fish offal and refuse thrown out, or hunt for themselves like wolves, after Arctic hares, lemmings or anything they can find.

In winter time, dogs are often the main food of the Esquimaux and as fat or oil is generally scarce, are eaten raw instead of cooked, oil being too valuable at this time to be wasted on dog. Its taste to the white man largely depends on one's hunger or digestive cravings. If half-starved, it is voted "just excellent." If not, it is "just dog," that's all. Yet, if the pangs of hunger gnaw one's vitals, repugnance, position in life, creed, superstition, opinions, likes and dislikes, self-respect, all give way to the cravings of an empty stomach; especially in that trackless great white desert called the "Distant Polar Regions."

Such is the life and existence of these, the sledge dogs of the north.

PART IV.

THE HUNTING DOG FAMILY

192 HUNTING DOGS.

A Worthy Fox Hound Aided with this Catch.

CHAPTER XIX.

AMERICAN FOX HOUNDS

THOSE who make a science of breeding and training fox hounds, and indulge in the chase for sport only, have a nearly identical standard of the ideal the country over. Even he who chases the fox for profit may find valuable information and interest in such a standard, even though they may be convinced that their hounds, though without pedigree, are capable dogs.

At a gathering of the foremost sportsmen of this country, in 1905, the following standard was fixed as ideal:

The American foxhound should be smaller and lighter in muscle and bone, than the English foxhound. Dogs should not be under 21 nor over $23\frac{1}{2}$ in., nor weigh more than 57 pounds. Bitches should not be under 20 nor over $22\frac{1}{2}$ inches nor weigh more than 50 pounds.

The head (value 15) should be of medium size with muzzle in harmonious proportions.

The skull should be rounded cross-wise with a slight peak, line of profile nearly straight, with sufficient stop to give symmetry to the head.

Ears should meet to within one inch of end of muzzle, should be thin, soft in coat, low set and closely pendant.

Eyes soft, medium size, and varying shades of brown. Nostrils slightly expanded. The head as a whole should denote hound character.

The neck (value 5) must be clean and of good length, slightly arched, strong where it springs from the shoulders and gradually tapering to the head, without trace of throatiness.

The shoulders (value 10) must be of sufficient length to give leverage and power, well sloped, muscular, but with clean run and not too broad.

Chest and back ribs (value 10). The chest should be deep for lung space, narrower in proportion to depth than the English hound, 28 inches in a 23½-inch hound being good. Well sprung ribs, back ribs should extend well back, a three-inch flank allowing springiness.

Back and loin (value 10) should be broad, short and strong, slightly arched.

The hindquarters and lower thighs (value 10) must be well muscled and very strong. The stifle should be low set, not too much bent, nor yet too straight, a happy medium.

The elbows (value 5) should set straight, neither in nor out.

Legs and feet (value 20) are of great importance. Legs should be straight and placed squarely under shoulder, having plenty of bone without clumsiness, strong pasterns well stood upon. Feet round, cat like, not too large, toes well knuckled, close and compact, strong nails, pad thick, tough and indurated by use.

Color and coat (value 5. Black, white and tan are preferable, though the solids and various pies are permissible. Coat should be rough and course without being wiry or shaggy.

Symmetry (value 5). The form of the hound should be harmonious thruout. He should show his blood quality and hound character in every aspect and movement. If he scores high in other properties, symmetry is bound to follow.

The stern (value 5) must be strong in bone at the root, of a medium length, carried like a sabre on line with the spine and must have a good brush. A docked stern shall not disqualify, but simply handicap according to extent of docking.

SUMMARY.

Head 15, neck 5, shoulders 10, chest and back ribs 10, hindquarters and lower thighs 10, back and loin 10, elbows 5, legs and feet 20, color and coat 5, stern 5, symmetry 5. Total 100.

THE GREY HOUND.

Without doubt, the grey hound, bred almost solely for speed, is the fleetest runner on earth.

In a general way it may be said that the grey hound pursues by sight only, yet some ex-

Good Specimens.

perienced hunters will contend that they can follow a fairly warm trail successfully, if trained to it. It is not natural for them, however, to take and follow an old track until the game is started, but what they lack in that way is made up in speed.

It has been a favorite practice for decades

AMERICAN FOX HOUNDS.

to take advantage of his speed, by crossing with other strains, resulting in courage, tenacity and trailing powers, very useful in several kinds of hunting.

This type of dog, either pure bred or crossed lends himself readily to deer, wolf, fox or rabbit chasing, and is especially successful if hunted in company with good trailers. The latter start the game when the grey hound goes forward and effects a capture, or so interferes with progress, that the other dogs come up and finish the work.

A bit of practical talk on the subject from the pen of a grey hound enthusiast is appended:

I have always had grey hounds. If they are let run with the track hounds when they are young they soon learn to take a track, run away from the pack and catch the game. I have some one-half grey hound and one-half bloodhound or fox hound. No better dogs living. Great fighters, stay as long as the game runs. This kind are good bear dogs. I keep live 'coon to train pups on and commence to train them at 4 or 5 months old. The older they get the longer races I give them.

SCOTCH DEER HOUND.

An excellent deer hound is half scotch deer hound and one-half grey hound, and I will say there is no breed called stag hound, writes a well informed Canadian deer hunter. All that claim that name are overgrown fox hounds used in England for that purpose. Thompson Gray in "Dogs of Scotland," written in 1890, says that the first mention of the Scotch deer hound was in "Pitcotts History of Scotland." It is of the same family as the grey hound and has been spoken of by early writers as the Rough Scotch Grey Hound.

He is more massive, is about three inches taller than the grey hound and has a rough coat. His vocation is to course the stag and the deer. He, like the grey hound must not use his nose when hunting his quarry and for this reason great speed is absolutely necessary. His head is somewhat longer and wider across the skull than that of the grey hound and the hair on the sides of the lip form a mustache. Small ears are a sign of good breeding. They should be set on high and at the back of the skull and be semi-erect when at attention.

The coat is hard in texture, without any silkiness. The color most admired is blue grizzle with its various shades but brindle and fawn, either light or dark are admirable. There should be no white on any part of the body. As to formation, he should be made on the same lines as the grey hound.

AMERICAN FOX HOUNDS.

THE BLOOD HOUND.

The original and oldest of the hound family is the blood hound. He takes his name from

Blood Hound.

having originally been used to track wounded animals to their lairs. Their fame to the public is based on their use as man trailers, which gained more notice at about the time of the Civil War than before or since. There is considerable question as to their infallibility and powers in this direction. While nearly any dog can, if he wishes, trail a human being, and while the blood hound is the best scented of the dog family, it is rather doubtful if all the things that have been written about the blood hounds and slave fugitives are true.

Bloodhounds are known under several names, such as, Cuban, Siberian, St. Hubert blood hounds, etc.

Civil authorities and detectives, the country over, employ the blood hounds to trail criminals, or rather ostensibly to bring them to justice. Rarely do they succeed in actually capturing a fleeing culprit, however, if he has passed over sections trampled over by many other people.

The blood hound, as has been mentioned before, is quite useful in breeding hunting dogs for specific purposes.

Some light of experience is furnished us by a Pennsylvania breeder, as follows:

In regard to blood hounds or a cross between the blood hound and fox hound, they are good hunters on wolf, fox, 'coon and bear. In fact, they are all around good dogs, great fighters on game. They are tough, active, will stand a long run and come home and not seem to be tired.

The blood hound is a good man as well as an animal hunter. They will stand the longest races and not tire. In fifty years breeding from the best, these dogs are all that are needed in a hound dog.

On the same subject a Western brother says:

I have bred dogs for 55 years from most of the kennels in this country, England and other countries. I like English blood hound or one-half hound and one-half fox hound. They are sharp scented, fast runners, good stayers, good fighters and game for fox and wolf hunting.

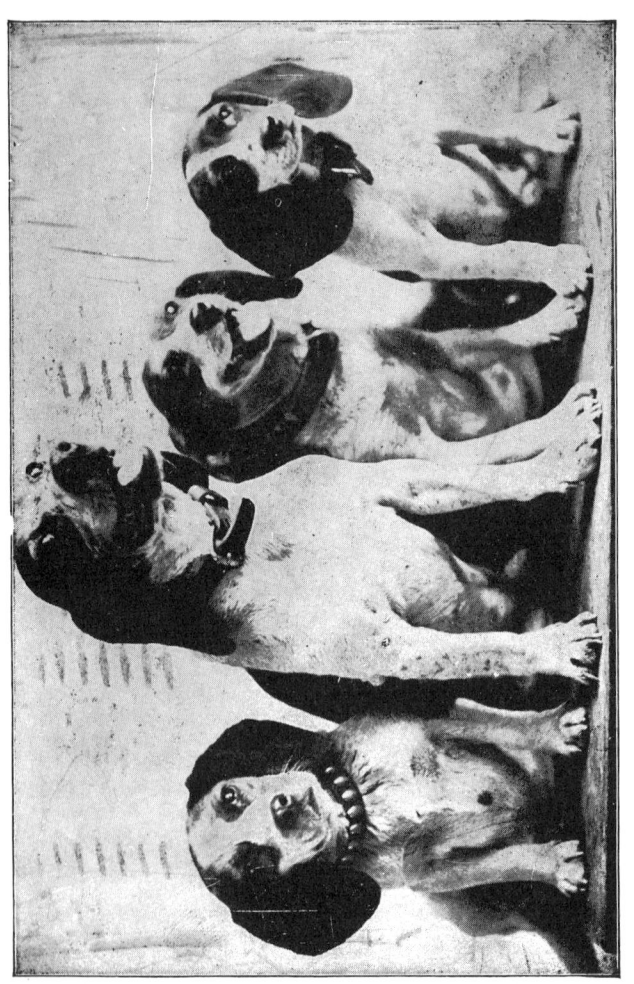

"As Pretty as a Picture." (Beagles.)

CHAPTER XXI.

THE BEAGLE DACHSHUND AND BASSET HOUNDS.

"A few years ago I gave up the large hound for the beagle hound, as I hunt rabbit a good deal now and I find it good sport with the right kind of beagles," writes a beagle enthusiast of the middle west, "but, of course, they are just like fox hounds or any other breed of dogs, many of them would be better training themselves in the happy hunting grounds. The main thing is to get the right strain of beagles, of which there are several. Champion Bannerman, imported by J. Crane, Esq., about 1884, has had a great influence towards producing the smaller size. Of course every man to his opinion as to size. Some prefer the small, while others the larger size. The importation by General Rowett, of Carlinsville, Ill., which has been known since as the Rowett strain, when it comes to beauty and hunting qualities combined, are very good, in fact, are among the best. The blue cap strain imported into the country by Captain William Ausheton from the kennels of Sir Arthur Ashburnham along in the seventies. This strain seems to have a stronger love for the scent of the rabbit than anything else.

By crossing strains it is possible to get beagles with a fierce hunting disposition, that will hunt and fight anything that wears fur, keen scent (remember the beagle is strong in the blood hound blood) wide chest, heavy bone, round fat feet that can put up a hard day's work every day.

THE DACHSHUND

We are indebted to Mr. William Loeffler for the following comprehensive, entertaining special article on the little understood Dachshund:

Of the many breeds of dogs in existence, none have gained more friends and won more hearts and a stronger hold in American home in a comparative short time than the Dachshund.

Those who have not seen a single specimen and are entirely ignorant regarding his characteristics, know him by continued caricature.

For centuries back he was the most favored pet of German aristocracy, carefully guarded and upheld in his purity, and it was only occasionally that an outsider received a specimen. A gift of a Dachshund was considered a token of high esteem.

Though he has not lost a particle of his prestige in this respect, and has strong admirers

True Dachshund Specimens.

in the royal families of Europe, he is rapidly becoming a cosmopolitan; with his little crooked legs he now travels over many lands, making friends wherever he lands.

At all times Dachshunde were in charge of professional hunters, who developed their instinct for hunting wonderfully, and the courage, endurance and strength exhibited in pursuing their game is astonishing and marvelous.

The long body, short and muscular legs, the entire strength being centered in his deep chest, indicate that he is intended for work under ground.

To attack a badger or a fox in his own burrow requires bravery of a high degree, especially as the dog is in most cases much smaller than his game. He relies upon the strength of his jaws and his wonderfully developed set of teeth for his work and does not snap or bite at random, but his attack is usually well aimed and effective.

The game-keeper's duty is to destroy all enemies of the game intrusted to his care, consequently foxes, badgers, minks and other vermin are at all times subject to extermination, and the Dachshund is his untiring and able assistant in this work.

His scenting power is of the keenest and he will locate his prey very quickly when he strikes a trail. A fox generally leaves his burrow when the dog enters his domain and falls a victim to the gunner's aim; not so with the badger, who crawl into a corner of his burrow, and two dogs in most cases attack him from different entries, and finally crowd him so that he will stay at bay. The location of the badger can easily be given by the barking of the dogs, and the hunter digs down with pick and spade, when the ground permits such work, until the badger can be seen. By means of a fork pushed over his neck the badger is held and captured.

The Dachshund is also invaluable for finding wounded deer; for which purpose the hunter usually chains the dog, who then leads his master over the trail to locate the game.

At home the Dachshund's disposition changes entirely; he is now a most affectionate and docile animal, and shows by his every expression his attachment for his master and his family. His intelligence is surprising; as a watch or house dog he has few equals, the slightest disturbance will not escape his keen senses and the alarm is given. Most always one member of the family he selects as his special idol, in many cases a child, and it is amusing to watch him, how he does everything in his power to show his affection, following every step taken by his beloved friend. He will frolic for hours and never seem to tire or lose his good temper, and he is always on hand when wanted. He knows the friends of the family and never molests them, but he will not tolerate tramps.

The color of the Dachshund is of great variety, the original stock being black and tan, from which later developed chocolate and tan, gray and tan and single color red, ranging from fawn to dark mahogany red. The spotted Dachshund, such as black and tan as a ground color showing silver gray patches of irregular sizes throughout the black field is of comparatively recent development. Most all have short and glossy coats.

The unusual shape of this dog, combined with a beautiful color, the graceful and dignified walk, the aristocratic bearing, will draw the attention and admiration of every one who sees him.

THE BASSET HOUND.

The American beagle has a brother in France, called the Basset. He is slow, acute scenter and in general has characteristics in common with the beagle.

Those few dogs in this country erroneously called Basset hounds, (aside from a very few imported for bench show purposes) are doubtless resulted from beagle and mongrel crossed.

A Pure Pointer.

CHAPTER XXII.

POINTERS AND SETTERS. — SPANIELS.

IT is not within our province to dwell at length upon the subject of "bird" dogs. We will content ourselves with briefly pointing out some more salient points of appearance and character. Those who wish to make a study and follow extensively wing shooting, and raise and train suitable dogs for the purpose, may obtain books relating exclusively to that subject.

While adapted to the same purposes in the field, there are differences in the appearance and methods of pointers and setters that give rise to two distinct classes.

In the field, if we may take for granted the claims of men long schooled in wing shooting, we may say in a general way, that the pointer excels in woods -- heavy cover, and brushy sections. In such places a slower dog is required as well as one that willingly hunts close to the shooter.

For work in open fields or over prairie land, the setter is perhaps better suited, because he, as a rule, "has greater speed, wider range, greater endurance and staying qualities. If retrieving from water came into play, the setter also would have the preference. As to which of the two breeds has the best nose, and which is the better bird finder, nothing can be said with a degree of certainty — they are equal, but there

Royal Sports.—Pointers in Action.

is a vast difference in individuals. The same is true as to retaining inculcated training."

The pointer is the older breed, being a product of the middle ages. He bobs up, ever and anon, in the history of hunting down to the present. There has been now and again some inclination to cross the pointer and fox hounds, among huntsmen, some claiming even in this day that it improves either type of dog for his given duties. Purists, however, insist on keeping them pure and undefiled.

In appearance the pointer is larger than the setter, and gives one an impression of solidity and strength; his coat should be soft and mellow, but not absolutely silky. The hair is short and straight.

The setter's coat should be long, straight and silky (a slight wave is admissible) which should be the case with the breeches and fore legs, which, nearly down to the feet, should be well feathered. The color may be either white and black, white and orange, white and lemon, white and liver, or black, white and tan; those without heavy patches on the body, but flecked all over, called Belton, preferred."

There is, as in most other questions of hunting and shooting experiences, wide difference of opinion as to the relative values of the two breeds for practical field work and bench purposes.

The casual field shooter will not go wrong in selecting either kind, so long as he secures a creditable and really representative individual.

A distinct setter strain is the black and tan Gordon. Writes an authority: "The Gordon is a much heavier dog in all his parts than the English setter; coarser in skull, thicker in

POINTERS AND SETTERS — SPANIELS. 213

Setter.

shoulders and usually carrying lots of useless lumber. As a consequence he lacks the speed of his English brethren, and for this reason he is not a desirable field trial candidate, but as a steady, reliable dog, with more than average bird finding ability, he will always have a number of admirers."

The Irish setter is another interesting one of the setter family. He is not as popular in America as the others, though a handsome and capable performer. His color is red, with white on chest, throat or toes, or a small star on the forehead.

The manner of judging pedigreed field dogs has been reduced to an almost exact science. After all, however, all this is not for the casual hunter and many an embryo sportsman tramps the fields after capable, though not so high-toned dogs, and enjoys it all more than the nervous owner watching his dog in the field trial.

SPANIELS.

Spaniels are not utilized to any extent as hunting dogs in this country, although they are sometimes crossed to good avantage with other hunting dogs. About the water, the water spaniel is well adapted. For instance some spaniel blood in a mink dog is well worth considering.

POINTERS AND SETTERS — SPANIELS.

All of the spaniels, readily develop into retrievers, and this is their principal use at present, although they can be taught to hunt with considerable effect and judgment, where too much is not expected of them. They are lively, happy little workers, and on grouse in dense coverts, no dog possesses a better nose for the purpose. Their size, too, is against them for most practical purposes.

CHAPTER XXIII.

TERRIERS — AIREDALES.

PRACTICAL hunters have no interest in the numerous Terrier family, save perhaps two types.

We find those who urge the use of the terrier for some purposes. For instance, a Canadian brother has the following to say as to the Fox Terrier:

I like the hound, but give me a well trained fox terrier as his companion, and I will get most every fox. They have no trouble to hole in less than six hours, there is where the terrier shines and puts in his work. He will enter the hole and that is the end of Mr. Fox. Sometimes he will bring him out of the hole to kill him, but more often he will kill him, then bring him out. There are times when he kills one that he cannot get out, owing to a short bend or other obstruction in the hole. No doubt there will be many of the readers think this is a far-fetched claim, nevertheless it is true and many in this section can vouch for this statement.

The dozens of types of this interesting, though generally impracticable terrier family we

TERRIERS — AIREDALES. 217

pass over, permitting us to give wider attention to the one or two types that have earned recognition. The ugly, little Irish terrier is sometimes used to good advantage for crossing, where

The Fox Terrier—Useful in Many Ways.

heedless, reckless pluck is sought. These dogs are very game, yet remarkably good tempered with man. But they dearly love a fight, and have earned their commonly used nick-name "Dare-devils."

Thus lightly skipping over the whole family we come to a type that has earned notice in the hunting world, and is rapidly growing in popular favor.

THE AIREDALE.

First we cite a bit of practical testimony on

Airedale.

matter, from a gentleman who knows where-
  speaks:
    have found out that the pure Airedale
    nd the hound make the very best dogs
    lynx, mink, etc. Get a good Airedale

and a good hound and you will have a pair of hounds hard to beat. The airedale are great water dogs and very hard workers and easily trained to hunt any kind of game. They are full of grit and they fear nothing and are always ready to obey your command. I have hunted with them and found this breed of dog away ahead of the water spaniel, collie, etc. Once you own one you will never be without it.

"The Airedales were first imported into this country in 1897 or 1898, from England, and as companion and guard dogs, as well as hunters and retrievers have made wonderful strides, and are becoming more popular as they become better known. In disposition and intelligence they are unexcelled. They will guard their master's family night and day, but on the other hand are affectionate and kind to children. They are natural hunters of both large and small game, in which they need but little training, and have been used and worked as hunters and retrievers with much success, as they are easily taught and very intelligent. In size, the standard calls for males 45 pounds, females a little less. Color, black and badger gray with tan extremities.

We should name the Airedale as a promising bear dog. His grit, courage, staying quality and strength are all points of advantage in a dog that is expected to try conclusions with the hard-swatting bruin.

Also we frequently hear of noteworthy success of the Airedale in hunting and dispatching coyotes, coons, badger and bay-lynx, any one of which is capable of putting up a good fight. Also he is a hunter, retriever, trailer of coon, 'possum, bear, wildcat, mink, coyote, deer, lynx, fox or small game.

The tendency nowadays is to produce larger Airedales, which shall retain the terrier qualities. The practical callings upon the breed's usefulness seems to justify that he be bred over 50 pounds, rather than between 45 and 50 pounds, which has in the past been the aim.

One writer says that it was in the valley of the Aire river that the Otter hound was crossed with the Bull Terrier, that product was the Scotch terrier, that with the Scotch collie, that with the Pointer, and that with the Setter dog and then the standard having been secured, the crossing was discontinued. In that dale of the Aire, then, was the great breed of dogs first experimented upon, that made the Airedale.

CHAPTER XXIV.

SCOTCH COLLIES. HOUSE AND WATCH DOGS.

THE Scotch collie dog will make the best friend of all the dogs in the canine race, writes a collie admirer. Of all useful animals God gave to man what can excel the dog, at least with the stockmen; in affection no other dog can compare with him, he is a dog that every farmer needs. He has almost human intelligence, a pure bred collie can always be depended upon in sunshine or adversity. He can do his work in a manner that should put the average boy to shame. The pure bred Scotch Collies are of a kind and affectionate disposition and they become strongly attached to their master. There can be no friend more honest and enduring than the noble, willing and obedient thoroughbred Scotch Collie. As a devoted friend and faithful companion he has no equal in the canine race, he will guard the household and property day and night. The Scotch Collies are very watchful and always on the alert, while their intelligence is really marvelous.

At one year old they are able to perform full duty herding sheep, cattle and other **stock, at-**

tending them all day when necessary, keeping them together and where they belong and driving off all strange intruders. They learn to

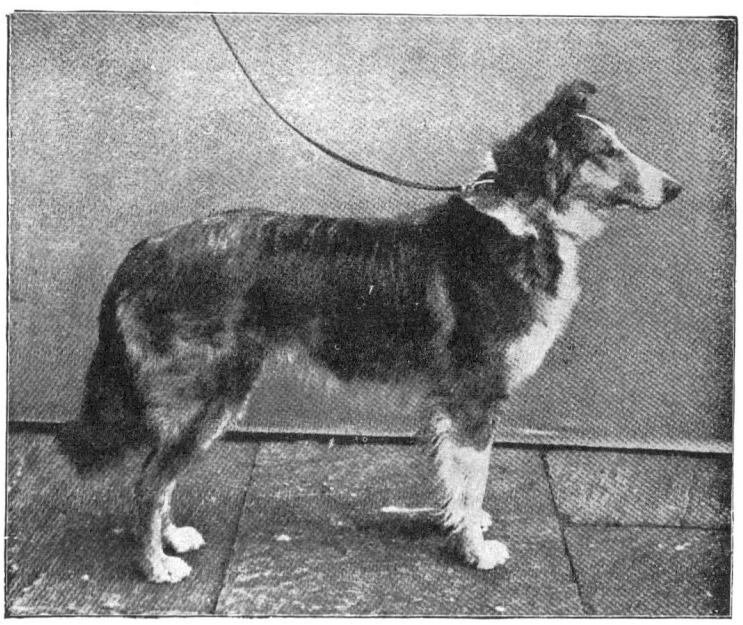

Collie.

know their master's animals from others in a very short time, and a well-trained dog will gather them home and put each into its right stall. They have a dainty carriage and fine style, profuse silky hair of various colors.

Others incline to the conviction that practical purposes have been lost sight of in breeding, and that appearances have been sought to such an extent that the present day pure bred collies lack some of the attributes of intelligence and hardihood that made the collie famous. In view of this fact it is quite likely that for general purposes and certainly for hunting purposes, a dash of alien blood is advantageous.

The crossed collie, or the well-known shepherd dog, so common to the farm, are very often used with success in all forms of night hunting. There are some who go so far as to maintain that the shepherd or a cross of shepherd and fox hound are ideal for coon, rabbit and squirrel hunting.

The use of these dogs as sheep herders has deteriorated in this country, although they are still bred for practical purposes with marked success in parts of England.

HOW TO TRAIN A COLLIE.

The best way to make a start is to get a pure-bred puppy from a good working strain. To gain the best results and secure the full worth of a Collie as a stock dog, I would say, take him as a little puppy.

There are many reasons why we favor the little puppy to the dog nearly or quite grown. Most collies are sensitive and suspicious and of fine temperament and this characteristic often makes them appear rather more cowardly than brave. A Collie that has been properly cared for and considerably handled during his puppyhood up to maturity should have plenty of courage. A puppy should never be permitted to have a place of refuge where he can run away and hide on hearing a slight noise or unusual disturbance of any kind, or at the sight of a stranger.

If he is kept under conditions where he can see all that may be going on, and in that way become familiar with active life, learning that noises and strange persons do not harm him, he will develop plenty of courage, without which there is but little hope of great usefulness.

First, teach him his name, and to come when you call him. Teach him to mind but always by kind methods. Let him love and trust you, gaining his affection by gentle treatment. He should be accustomed to the collar and chain when young, though it is much better to keep him in the yard than confined by a chain while he is growing. Teach him one thing at a time — to lie down and remain in that position until excused; to follow at your will, and stop at the word, to come in at once at command, and to turn to the right or left.

All these lessons can be easily managed by

use of a small cord and always using the appropriate word with emphasis. He should always be made to keep at your heels when out for a walk with you. In that way, after telling him to go to heel whenever he tries to run away, he will understand the word better when he goes with you to drive the cattle for the first time.

Let him keep back of the stock with you, while you drive the cattle to and from the field or pasture without undertaking to teach him, for as he learns by observation, he must have the example made plain. He will quickly show a desire to help and then you may take advantage of this act, encouraging him to help you, and after he has been with you a time or two, he will soon become a driver at the heel. Give him plenty of practice, and when he becomes a good driver at the heel, taking a positive interest in his work, he can then be easily taught to turn the cattle to the right or left, to head them off, stop them or go alone into the distant fields and bring the cattle to the stable.

He should never be allowed to drive the cattle fast for if once allowed to run them, he will become careless and develop a disposition to worry them.

Do not weary him with over-commanding nor notice every little mistake which unnoticed

Shepherd Puppies.

may not occur again. If you gain his affection and do not forget to tell him that he has been a good dog when he has done well for you, he will learn fast for he has a wonderful memory and never forgets the things he has learned to do. Thus we are amply repaid for the care and time used in making the lesson plain.

I might say a few words about feeding the puppy, as he should have good food when young. The first few months he should be fed on bread and milk, never giving him any meat at any time, and as he grows older, give him the bread dry and the milk as a drink. A comfortable sleeping place should also be given him. The best place is in the house or stable and he should be kept in at night at all times of the year.

You will find that a well looked after Collie is a valuable and life-long friend and helper.

HOUSE AND WATCH DOGS.

The Great Dane, Mastiff, St. Bernard, Newfoundland, Poodle, Dalmatian Chow-Chow, English and French Bulldog have their places and purposes, but are entirely outside the province of hunting dogs. Most hunters admire these noble beasts, but inasmuch as they have no practical importance or use to the hunter, detailed description is omitted.

CHAPTER XXV.

A FARMER HUNTER — HIS VIEWS.

I am a farmer by trade and a raccoon hunter for sport, and nothing but a fox hound for me, and the better his breeding is the better I like it. I don't care how much noise he makes if he is fast. I like a good tonguer. I only have four hounds at this writing. I have caught 27 'coon and 10 opossum. On the night of November 9th, some friends of mine went out 'coon hunting with me. They had three 'coon dogs and I had four, seven hounds in all. We went about two miles south of where I live to where we sometimes hunt the 'coon. The first thing when we got there the dogs struck a trail and treed on top of a hill with an old coal entry just below it.

We got up to the tree all right and could hear one of the dogs barking "treed" about one-half mile south, so I left the boys to attend to that tree and I went to the lone hound. He was barking up a large black oak in the corn field. I soon spied an eye up the tree and shot him out and down came Mr. 'Coon. I looked up in the tree again and saw two eyes. The little 20-gauge

A FARMER HUNTER — HIS VIEWS. 229

spoke again and down came 'coon No. 2. The other fellows did not have such good luck, as their coon got into the coal entry.

We then started on and the dogs caught another trail and gave us some music for about twenty minutes. When they barked treed we went over to them and there were six of the dogs barking up a bushy oak and the lone dog was barking about eighty rods west of there. One of the boys started up the tree and got only part way up when out jumps Mr. 'Coon. The dogs all went for him and out comes another 'coon and into the corn field he went just about at the top of his speed, and I guess he had no slow orders either by the way he was going the last time I saw him. We got a couple of the dogs after the runaway 'coon but he made a hole, so we then went to the lone dog and he had one up. We got that and started west. We had not gone far when the dogs struck another trail and they circled to the northwest of us, came around west and south and turned east. Just across the hollow from us was a large tree that Mr. 'Coon was trying to make but he couldn't get speed enough to make it, so the dogs caught him as he got to the bottom of the tree.

The lone dog was with them on that chase. We left our 'coon at a farmer's and started on. The dogs struck another trail and that 'coon got into a hole and he was safe, so we ate our lunch, rested a little while and started on west. The dogs hit another trail and went south about a mile and barked but not treed. We went to them and they had run this 'coon into a shallow hole in the corn field. We tried to get one of the dogs to pull him out but the 'coon got first hold every time, so we got a stick and dug in a little ways. We could then see Mr. 'Coon's eyes down in the hole. We sent three dogs in after him but they came out without him.

I had an old speckled hound we called Teddy. He went in and when he backed out he had company with him, and he seemed to think a great deal of his company, for he was hanging right on to him just as though he thought his company might leave him if he got a chance. Ted was doing all he could, but he got him up so the other dogs could see Mr. 'Coon's back and then he had plenty of help and the 'coon's troubles were soon over.

We then started northwest. The dogs were working a trail and they were puzzled on it; did not seem able to get away. There were a black oak and hazel bush where we were then, so we sat down to let the dogs work it out if they could. We were sitting within 10 feet of an oak tree, the lone dog came up, circles the tree and barks up, then three of the other dogs

A FARMER HUNTER — HIS VIEWS. 231

come up and start to bark. One of the boys says there might be a 'coon up that tree but I doubt it. Well, I said, when four good 'coon dogs bark up a tree at the same time, there is liable to be something up there, so up went one of the boys and down came Mr. 'Coon. We got him and the dogs were not long in starting another trail.

They started south but it was a cold one, but they struck right after Mr. 'Coon, and I guess they must have taken us a mile and a half on that trail to another patch of timber, and we were about a half a mile behind them when they barked treed. They had Mr. 'Coon up a tall red oak. We shot him out and soon had another trail going. They took this one south, and it was a warm one, right out into a corn field, and they caught him on the ground. We could hear the fracas and went to them as quick as possible, but we were not quick enough for they had killed Mr. 'Coon and we met them coming back. We went to where we thought they were when they caught the 'coon but we did not find the right place for we did not find that coon.

The dogs soon had another trail going and gave us some fine music for a little while and barked treed. We went to them and they had two 'coons up. We shot them out, and they soon had another one going south. It was getting pretty frosty about that time and they worked that trail about one hour south and west. We followed their music and they barked treed. We shot him out. That makes eleven 'coon and one killed in the field that we could not find. Now there may be some of the trappers that will think I have added a few 'coon to this hunt, but I have not. I have given you this 'coon hunt as near as it happened as I can remember, but we had seven as good 'coon dogs as you generally run across. I do not say seven of the best dogs ever went into the woods or the best in the United States, but they were 'coon dogs and fast ones.

It seems that about every man that has a 'coon dog or dogs and they tree a few 'coons, gets it into his head that nobody has a dog quite as good as his. I have one pair of hounds from a Williams bitch and a dog owned by Mr. Williams — Hodo is his name — but he is a pure Trigg dog. His pedigree runs back over forty years. One of Haiden C. Trigg's dogs, Trigg, is the most successful hound breeder in the United States today. He started on the old original American fox hound, these long eared fellows with a deep mellow voice, called by some nigger chasers, as they used them in the south for that purpose, and some dealers are selling the old American Fox Hound today for Ameri-

A FARMER HUNTER — HIS VIEWS.

can Blood Hounds. The only genuine blood hound we have is the English. See what the Trigg dog is today, short ears or much shorter than the dog Mr. Trigg started to improve on, with narrow muzzle, and stands up well with good feet and built on speedy lines, a red fox dog, and when he started on there were few of them that could hole a red fox inside of eight hours, and the Trigg dog of today will hole a red fox in a comparatively short time. Of course the fox they are running and the kind of country they have to run in, have a great deal to do with it. I run fox myself sometimes, or my hounds do rather.

Now I see some of the hunters like a still trailer, but I want to hear my dogs work and I want to know which way they are going, and when they begin to get away I can follow and keep in hearing of my dogs. I can tell by their baying just about what they are doing, if the trail is cold or warm, and can tell which way they are going. I wouldn't give a cent to hunt with dogs that couldn't make a little music when on the trail.

I see some of the brothers think nothing but a still trailer catches his 'coon on the ground. If you have fast trailers they will catch 'coon on the ground if they tongue every other jump. My dogs are all good tonguers and I often have them catch 'coon on the ground and big 'coon, not little young 'coon any more than old ones. A young 'coon will take to a tree quicker than an old one. I have got to see my first well bred 'coon hound that will still trail. I have never seen him yet, that is, a fox hound. I have tried shepherd and hound cross, bull dog and hound cross, and beagle and fox hound cross, but give me the pure bred fox hound every time for a 'coon dog, and I don't care how long his pedigree is either. Let me tell you, you cannot get a fox hound too fast for 'coon, the faster he is the better.

I read where a brother made the statement that you wanted a slow hound for a 'coon dog. Well, he may want a slow one, yet I am sure I do not. He goes on to say that a fast dog will run over the trail if the 'coon makes a short or square turn, the fast hound will run by and lose too much time finding the trail again. Let me tell you right here, the fast hound can't help but run over, but he knows right where he lost that trail. If he happens to circle the right way, he only has to make a half circle and he is off again. On the other hand, if he circles the other way he makes a full circle and hits the trail and is going just as fast as ever. If he has a good nose on him he has not lost four seconds. A fast hound will make that turn in a trail quicker

A FARMER HUNTER — HIS VIEWS.

every time than a slow one will. I have had both slow and fast and have hunted 'coons about 23 years. Am now a man 38 years old, and if I don't know what a hound is I sure never will.

I don't claim to know it all, for a man never gets too old to learn. He could learn something every day if he lived a thousand years, or for all time to come. There is no dog that will work a cold trail out like a good hound. He will work out a trail and tree a 'coon when a cur dog would pass right over the trail and pay no attention to it whatever. It must be the brothers that like the still trailers that never had a good 'coon hound, for I have never seen good 'coon dogs but I have seen the best ones wrapped up in a fox hound hide.

I have a black and tan hound that will fight for me at any time. I can't scuffle with any one outside of my own family for he will bite them just as quick as he can get close enough to them. I had to give him several hard whippings to make him quit rabbits. Now they don't bother him any when he is looking for 'coon with me at night. His father was the hardest dog to break off of rabbits that I ever broke, but when he was three years old he would not notice a rabbit at night but would trail them in the day time. He turned out to be a very valuable hound. He would retrieve as good as a retriever on land or in water, would catch any hog that I told him to catch and hold it until I told him to let it go. I could point out any chicken I wanted him to catch and he would get it for me and would not hurt the chicken any.

Some people think a hound don't know anything but trail, but a good hound is a very smart dog and a poor hound is about as worthless a dog as you can find. Take the hound as a breed and I must say they are a noble breed. The fox hound requires, I think, more exercise than any other breed of dogs. I have a 25 gallon caldron. I put most any kind of meat that I can get, beef, horse flesh, 'coon, when there is one that is pretty badly bruised up, pork or any kind of meat that is not decomposed, and put it into this caldron. Of course, I put water in first then put in my meat and boil until it will all stir off the bone. I then take all the bones out and stir in corn meal until I have enough so that when the meal is done it will be a very stiff mush. When it is done and cooled off you can take it out in chunks. Use no salt, if any, very little, as a very little salt will physic a dog.

I sometimes bake corn bread for the dogs for a change, which makes a good food for them but not so strong a food as the other. I think a hound will do more running and keep in better order on that mush with meat than any food you can give them. Of course, if a person has but one dog, he can generally get enough from the house scraps from the table, but when you have a dozen or so you will have to get your dog food elsewhere. In warm weather this mush will sour in a few hours, but in cold weather it will keep sweet. I feed my dogs once a day when they are idle, but when I am hunting them I feed them twice a day. Feed each dog by himself.

Now as to their sleeping places, if you can let your dogs run loose, and they will find warm places to sleep, with plenty of bedding in the barn or other out buildings where the ventilation is good, but no drafts of air to blow on them, that is the best place for them. I keep part of my dogs tied up, as they would be off hunting if I let them run loose. For those I use on the chain I use a 20-foot chain. Build a good, warm dog house with a shingle roof, an individual house for one dog. Cut a hole that he can get thru easily and then tack some burlap just above the hole and let it hang down over the hole. When it is cold weather I leave it down, but when it is pleasant I fasten it up so that it leaves the hole open. The air can get thru the burlap but it breaks the wind off of the dog and keeps the snow from blowing in on his nest, or rain if it is raining. He can go out and in when the burlap is down.

Another easy way to make a good place for a dog is cut a hole in the side of a building that has a good roof, and put a box large enough so that it will give your dog plenty of room right tight up against the inside of the building where you cut the holes thru. Knock one side of your box out and put it to the hole on inside of building. Put your burlap on the outside at the hole as before described, and you have a fine place for your dog. Make the hole just large enough so he can get thru it easily, and cut it high enough so that when he lays down in the box, the bottom of the hole will be above the dog. Give your dog good, clean bedding at least once a week. Twice a week is not too often. Use some disinfectant about two or three times a month inside of dog house. The best cure for mange that I have ever used, or for sores to heal them is black gun powder, powdered sulphur and lard, mixed and well rubbed in. It is a sure cure for mange. It will soon kill the germs, if properly applied.

I notice where a brother, in telling how to break a young dog to tree 'coon said, to let the 'coon chew the dog for a while, help the 'coon, let him eat the dog for about 20 minutes and the dog would go to hunting them to get revenge, or something to that effect. Now it is my opinion that the dog would not want any more revenge as he would get a plenty right there, and the chances are that he would ever after be afraid of a 'coon, if he were a pup and got that kind of treatment. Help your dog kill a 'coon whenever you can, if you can do it without danger to the dog. I never let my dogs kill a 'coon when it can be avoided. If I can find the 'coon with my light in the tree I shoot him out, and then sometimes he has plenty of fight in him when he comes down. Other times he is dead when he hits the ground.

Any one of my dogs will kill a 'coon if necessary, but they don't get the chance very often. There has been a few times that I let them kill the 'coon, when I could have killed him myself, when there were some of the boys with me that wanted to see them kill the 'coon, but it is tiresome work on a dog to kill a 'coon, harder a great deal than treeing one. My dogs will not stay at a hole unless the 'coon is very close to the top of the ground, as where I hunt there are a great many old coal entries and it would be a nuisance to have them bark at such places as you could not get them out, so I never encourage them to stay at a hole when they run one in.

I have seen some discussion about the size of 'coons. The largest 'coon I ever caught weighed 30 pounds. He measured from the tip of his tail to the end of his nose, 4 feet and 4 inches. I caught another one last winter that weighed 25 pounds and measured four feet and 2 inches from his nose to the end of his tail.

I catch a good many that weigh over 20 pounds. Another thing I want to tell you is this, in over 20 years of 'coon hunting I have never cut a tree down to get a 'coon. There is too much of that kind of work done. Where are all of the 'coons going to stay when you get all of the den trees cut down? I want to ask you where is the land owner that wants 'coon hunters cutting his timber down? Think of cutting a fine, large tree down because it has a hole in it with a 'coon inside. If I get a 'coon in such a tree and can't climb it, I just call the dogs away from the tree and let him go until some other time. I make it my business to go that way again some night, and the chances are I get that same 'coon in such a tree and can't climb it, I just tree a head of Mr. 'Coon if I can, and he goes up some tree that I can get him out of when he sees he is cut off from his den tree, and the tree is left for the next 'coon that comes along. So, brothers, please cut the tree cutting out, as it is for your own good to let those kind of trees stand if you want to hunt 'coon. When you go around thru the timber destroying it, some one is going to call a halt

A FARMER HUNTER — HIS VIEWS. 241

on you, and on the other hand it is not at all necessary to cut the timber to get the 'coon, and the tree is undoubtedly worth more to the man that own the land than the 'coon is to you

Of course, if the owner of the tree gives you permission to cut the tree, that clears you on that score, but after the tree is down, you will never find another 'coon in that tree.

CHAPTER XXVI.

DESCRIPTIVE TABLE OF TECHNICAL TERMS AS APPLIED TO THE DOG.

The following table of definitions are used descriptive of the parts of the dog's anatomy, and are used and understood generally by professionals:

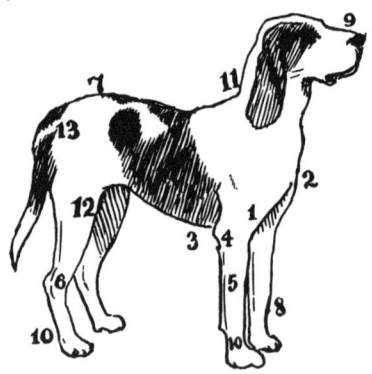

(*The numbers refer to the picture.*)

Apple-headed. — Skull round instead of flat on top.
1. ARM.
    Blaze. — A white mark up the face.
    Brush. — The tail of a Collie, or any bushy tail.

TABLE OF TECHNICAL TERMS, ETC. 243

2. BRISKET. — The part of the body between the chest and the neck. Front part of chest.

   Butterfly-nose. — A spotted nose.

   Button-ear. — An ear which falls over in front, concealing the inside, as in Fox-Terriers.

   Broken-up Face. — Refers more particularly to the face of the Bulldog or Toy Spaniel, and comprises the receding nose, or lay-back, deep stop, and wrinkle.

   Burr. — The inside of the ears.

   Breeching. — The tan-colored hairs on the back of the thighs of a Black-and-tan Terrier.

   Beefy. — Big, beefy hind-quarters.

   Cat-foot. — A short, round foot, with the knuckles high and well developed; like a cat's, short, round and compact.

3. CHEST. — The chest of a dog must not be confounded with the brisket; the breast or chest extends between the fore-legs from the brisket to the belly.

   Cheeky. — When the cheek bumps are strongly defined; thick in cheek.

   Chaps or Chops. — The pendulous lips of the Bull-dog; the foreface of a Bulldog.

Cobby. — Well ribbed up; short and compact.

Cloddy or Cobby. — Thick-set, short-coupled and low in stature.

Couplings. — The length or space between the tops of the shoulder-blades and tops of the hip-joints, or buckle-bones. A dog is accordingly spoken of as long or short "in the couplings."

Cow-hocked. — The hocks turning inward; hocks that turn in, like those of a cow.

Cushion. — Fulness in the top lips.

Crook-tail. — The crooked tail of a Bulldog.

Crank-tail. — Same as above.

Culotte. — The feather on the thighs, as in the Schipperke and Pomeranian.

Character. — The combination of points contributing to the whole make-up and giving to a dog that which is desired in his particular variety.

Corky. — Compact and active looking; springy and lively in action.

Dew-claws. — The extra claws found occasionally on the legs of all breeds, but especially of the St. Bernard; the superfluous claws inside the hind-leg just above the foot.

TABLE OF TECHNICAL TERMS, ETC. **245**

Dewlap. — Pendulous skin under the throat as in case of Blood-hound.

Dish-faced. — This term describes a dog whose nasal bone is higher at the nose than at the stop — a feature not infrequently seen in pointers.

Dudley-nose. — A flesh-colored nose.

Domed Skull. — Round skull.

Deep in Brisket. — Deep in chest; deep from withers to point where chest and brisket meet.

4. ELBOW. — The joint at the top of the forearm.

Elbows Out or "Out at Elbows." — This term defines itself. Bulldogs and Dachshunde are desirable with elbows so shaped, but it may occur as a fault through weakness.

Expression. — The expression of a dog is largely but not wholly determined by the size, angular position, and degree of prominence of the eye. For instance in a St. Bernard the eye is small, somewhat sunken, showing a little haw. This gives a dignified and rather benevolent expression. "Collie expression" depends largely on the angle at which eyes are set to each other.

Feather. — The fringe of hair on the back of legs of some breeds, notably Setters, Spaniels, and Sheep-dogs. The feathering on legs, as in the Setter and Spaniel.

Flag. — The tail of a Setter.

Flews. — The chops, or overhanging lips of the upper jaw. The term is chiefly applied to hounds or other deep-mouthed dogs. The lips.

5. FOREARM.—This makes the principal length of the fore-leg and extends from elbow to pastern.

Frill. — The long hair on the brisket of some dogs, and especially of the Collie. The profuse hair under the neck.

Frog-face or Down-face. — Nose not receding.

Flat-sided. — Flat in ribs; opposite of well-ribbed up.

Grizzle. — A bluish-gray color.

Hare-foot. — Foot like that of a hare, long and narrow.

Haw. — The red inside eyelid, usually hidden, but visible in Bloodhounds and St. Bernards; the red membrane inside the lower eyelid.

6. HOCKS. — The lower joint of hind-leg.

Height. — The height of a dog is measured

TABLE OF TECHNICAL TERMS, ETC. **247**

    at the shoulder, bending the head gently down. The proper method is to place the dog on level ground close by a wall, and to lay a flat rule across his shoulders so as to touch the wall; then measure to the point touched by the rule.

7. HUCKLE-BONES. — Tops of the hip-joints. The space between these and the tops of the shoulders is called the couplings.

    Harlequin. — Pied, mottled, or patchy in color.

8. KNEE. — The joint attaching the fore-pasterns and the forearm.

    Kink-tail. — A tail with a single break or kink in it.

    Leather. — The ears *i. e.*, the loose visible part of them.

    Layback. — Receding nose.

    Loins. — That part of the anatomy of the dog between the last rib and hindquarters.

    Long in Flank. — Long in back and loins.

    Lumber. — Superfluous flesh.

    Mask. — The dark muzzle of a Mastiff or Pug.

    Mane. — The profuse hair on top of neck.

    Merle. — A bluish-gray color splashed with black.

Monkey-faced. — *See* Dish-faced.

9. NASAL BONE.

Occiput. — The prominent bone at the back or top of the skull; particularly prominent in Bloodhounds; the bony bump on the top of the head.

Overshot. — The upper teeth projecting over the lower. This fault in excess makes a dog pig-jawed. The top jaw protruding beyond the lower jaw.

Out at Shoulders. — Shoulders set on outside, as in the Bulldog.

Out at Elbows. — Elbows turning out.

10. PASTERN. — The lowest section of the leg, below the knee or hock respectively, usually only applied to those joints on front legs.

Pig-jawed. — The upper jaw protruding over the lower, so that the upper incisor teeth are in advance of the lower, an exaggeration of an over-shot jaw.

Pily. — A peculiar quality of coat found on some dogs, which show on examination a short woolly jacket next the skin, out of which springs the longer visible coat. This short woolly coat is "pily." When an ordinary coat is described as pily, it means that it is soft and woolly, instead of hard.

TABLE OF TECHNICAL TERMS, ETC.

Prick Ear. — (*See* Tulip ear). An erect ear; not turned down or folded.

Plume. — The tail of a Pomeranian.

Pad. — The under portion or sole of the foot.

Penciling. — The black marks or streaks divided by tan on the toes of a Black-and-tan Terrier.

Rose-ear. — An ear of which the tip turns backward and downward, so as to disclose the inside of the ear.

13. RUMP-BONE.

Ring-tail. — A tail curving round in circular fashion.

Roach Back or Arched Loins.— The arched or wheel formation of loin, as in a Greyhound, Dachshunde, Dandie Dinmont Terrier, and Bulldog.

Racy. — Slight in build and leggy, as in the Greyhound or Whippet.

Septum.—The division between the nostrils.

11. SHOULDERS. — Top of the shoulder-blades, the point at which the height of a dog is measured.

Splay-foot. — A flat, awkward front foot, usually turned outward; and the opposite of "Cat-foot."

Stern. — The tail.

12. STIFLE-JOINTS. — Stifles. The joints of hind-leg next above the hocks.

Stop. — The indentation across the skull between the nose and the eyes. This feature is strongly developed in Bulldogs, Pugs and short-faced Spaniels, and considerably so in many other dogs. The step or indentation between the forehead and nose.

Snipy. — Too pointed in muzzle.

Semi-prick Ear. — An erect ear of which the end falls over forward.

Sickle-tail. — A tail forming a semicircle, like a sickle.

Short-coupled. — Short in back and loins.

Shelly. — Too narrow and light in body.

Second Thighs. — The muscular development between stifle-joint and hock.

Style. — Showy, spirited, or gay demeanor.

Tulip-ear. — An upright or prick ear.

Topknot. — The hair on top of the head, as in the Irish Water Spaniel, Dandie Dinmont, and Bedlington Terrier.

Throatiness. — Overmuch loose skin or flesh under throat.

Twist. — The curled tail of a Pug.

Trace. — The dark mark down the back of a Pug.

Tucked-up. — Tucked-up loin, as in the Greyhound.

Tricolor. — Black, tan and white.

Thumb Marks. — The round, black spots on the forelegs of a Black-and-tan Terrier.

Timber. — Bone.

Undershot. — The lower incisor teeth, projecting beyond the upper, as in Bulldogs. The under jaw protruding beyond the upper jaw.

Upright Shoulders. — Shoulders that are set in an upright, instead of an oblique position; not laid back.

Vent. — The tan colored hair below root of tail.

Varmint Expression. — As in the eye of the Fox Terrier, which is free from Haw, is not Sunken, is round but rather small than large, and set horizontally, not obliquely, giving a keen, rather "cussed" look.

Wall-eye. — A blue mottled eye.

Wrinkle. — Loose folding skin over the skull.

Wheaten. — Pale yellowish color.

Withers. — Same as 11.

CANADIAN WILDS

Tells about the Hudson Bay Company, Northern Indians and their Modes of Hunting, Trapping, in a by-gone era.

This book is from the pen of a Hudson Bay Officer (Martin Hunter), who had over 40 years experience in Canada from 1863 to 1903. He married an Indian woman and was closely associated with her people. He accompanied the Indians on their trapline and on their hunting trips and participated in these activities. He gleaned a vast store of hunting and trapping lore in this way and from the stories told around the camp fires. This big book contains 277 pages of interesting and informative reading of this phase of Indian life. There are 37 chapters as follows:

I. The Hudson's Bay Company
II. The "Free Trader"
III. Outfitting Indians
IV. Trackers of the North
V. Provisions for the Wilderness
VI. Forts and Posts
VII. About Indians
VIII. Wholesome Foods
IX. Officer's Allowances
X. Inland Packs
XI. Indian Mode of Hunting Beaver
XII. Indian Mode of Hunting Lynx and Marten
XIII. Indian Mode of Hunting Foxes
XIV. Indian Mode of Hunting Otter and Musquash
XV. Remarkable Success
XVI. Things to Avoid
XVII. Anticosti and its Furs
XVIII. Chiseling and Shooting Beaver
XIX. The Indian Devil
XX. A Tame Seal
XXI. The Care of Blistered Feet
XXII. Deer Sickness
XXIII. A Case of Nerve
XXIV. Amphibious Combats
XXV. Art of Pulling Hearts
XXVI. Dark Furs
XXVII. Indians are Poor Shots
XXVIII. A Bear in the Water
XXIX. Voracious Pike
XXX. The Brass Eyed Duck
XXXI. Good Wages Trapping
XXXII. A Pard Necessary
XXXIII. A Heroic Adventure
XXXIV. Wild Oxen
XXXV. Long Lake Indians
XXXVI. Den Bears
XXXVII. The Mishap of Ralson

A. R. HARDING PUB. CO.

2878 E. Main St.   Columbus, Ohio 43209

FOX TRAPPING

A Book of Instructions Telling How to Trap, Snare and Shoot. A Valuable Book for Trappers.

THE Author in his introduction to this book says: If all the methods as explained in this book had been studied out by one man and he began trapping when Columbus discovered America, he would be far from completed. The methods given in this book are largely from old and experienced trappers who have given their own successful methods, enabling the trapper of little experience with fox to be like them able to outwit.

Trappers who have caught the valuable silver fox as well as those who have caught cross, red and gray have furnished the Author with information for this book so that trappers from any section will find a method or methods that can be used. The red fox, however, is the one that most sets describe, yet what is a good method for one species is pretty sure to be for others.

This book contains about 50 illustrations, nearly 200 pages and twenty-two chapters as follows:

I. General Information.
II. Baits and Scents.
III. Foxes and Odor.
IV. Chaff Method Set.
V. Traps and Hints.
VI. All Round Land Set.
VII. Snow Set.
VIII. Trapping Red Fox.
IX. Red and Gray.
X. Wire & Twine Snare.
XI. Trap, Snare, Shooting and Poison.
XII. My First Fox.
XIII. Tennessee Trapper's Method.
XIV. Many Good Methods
XV. Fred and the Old Trapper.
XVI. Experienced Trapper Tricks.
XVII. Reynard Outwitted.
XVIII. Fox Shooting.
XIX. A Shrewd Fox.
XX. Still Hunting the Fox.
XXI. Fox Ranches.
XXII. Steel Traps.

This book has been a wonderful help to many in outwitting sly foxes—silver, cross, red and gray. Some sets had best be made in advance of the trapping season so as to become "weather beaten"—old looking.

A. R. HARDING, Pub. Co., 2878 E. Main St., Columbus, Ohio 43209

Bee Hunting

A BOOK OF VALUABLE INFORMATION FOR BEE HUNTERS. Tells How to Line Bees to Trees, Etc.

The following is taken from the Author's Introduction to BEE HUNTING

MANY books on sports of various kinds have been written, but outside of an occasional article in periodicals devoted to bee literature, but little has been written on the subject of Bee Hunting. Therefore, I have tried in this volume—Bee Hunting for Pleasure and Profit—to give a work in compact form, the product of what I have learned along this line during the forty years in nature's school room.

Brother, if in reading these pages, you find something that will be of value to you, something that will inculcate a desire for manly pastime and make your life brighter, then my aim will have been reached.

The book contains 13 chapters as follows:

I. Bee Hunting.
II. Early Spring Hunting.
III. Bee Watering—How to Find Them.
IV. Hunting Bees from Sumac.
V. Hunting Bees from Buckwheat.
VI. Fall Hunting.
VII. Improved Mode of Burning.
VIII. Facts About Line of Flight.
IX. Baits and Scents.
X. Cutting the Tree and Transferring.
XI. Customs and Ownership of Wild Bees
XII. Benefactors and Their Inventions.
XIII. Bee Keeping for Profit.

This book contains 80 pages, paper cover.

A.R.HARDING, Pub., 2878 E. Main St., Columbus, Oh. 43209

Camp and Trail Methods

*Interesting Information for All Lovers of Nature—
the Outdoors. What to Take and What to Do.*

THE author, E. Kreps, who has spent several years in various parts of North America camping, hunting, and trapping, says: "A life in the open air calls for knowledge which a very large number of human beings, because of their environments, cannot gain, except when the same is imparted by some more fortunate one who has learned it from experience. There are many who live this outdoor life and these old seasoned woodsmen know, perhaps, all that is contained in this book, but there are others, a much larger number, who do not know the many things relating to outdoor life, which it is almost necessary that one should be well ecquainted with when he or she make their first trip into the fastnesses of Mother Nature.

"There are many books on woodcraft, written by sportsmen, fishermen, and campers, but only a few of these books were written by practical woodsmen and for people who want to belong to that class. Such books are intended for the big game hunter, or the fisherman who goes for a short stay into some easily accessible location, well equipped and with a guide who does all the work and looks after the comfort of those whom he has in charge. This book is a decided departure from that class, as it not only gives the information needed by the tourist and summer camper, but gives special attention to the needs of those practical ones whose calling, whatever it may be, leads them into the wilds and holds them there at all times of the year; the hunter, the fisherman, the trapper, the prospector, the surveyor; all these and many ohers will find much valuable information in this book."

This practical books contains 274 pages and 68 illustrations. There are 19 chapters as follows:

I. Pleasures and Profits of Camping.
II. Selecting a Camp Outfit.
III. Clothing for the Woods.
IV. Pack Straps, Pack Sacks and Pack Baskets.
V. Cooking Utensils, Beds and Bedding.
VI. Firearms.
VII. Hunting Knives and Axes.
VIII. Tents and Shelters.
IX. Permanent Camps.
X. Canoes and Hunting Boats.
XI. Snowshoes and Their Use
XII. Snowshoe Making.
XIII. Skis, Toboggans and Trail Sleds.
XIV. Provisions and Camp Cookery.
XV. Bush Travel.
XVI. Traveling Light.
XVII. Tanning Furs and Buckskins.
XVIII. Preserving Game, Fish and Hides.
XIX. Miscellaneous Suggestions.

As the author says, this book is so written that it is of value to anyone who camps or goes upon the "trail." Read the chapter headings carefully. This book tells what to take and what to do. The book is paper bound, printed on good paper, size 5x7 inches.

A. R. Harding Pub. Co.   2878 E. Main St.—Columbus, Ohio 43209

Ginseng and Other Medicinal Plants

A Valuable Book for Growers and Collectors of Wild Medicinal Plants—Tells How to Grow, Medicinal Uses, Etc.

THIS book, Revised Edition, contains 367 pages and about 100 illustrations, 40 being Ginseng, showing this plant in various stages of development, both cultivated and wild; also roots of different sizes and quality with explanation of value, etc. Also 20 illustrations of Golden Seal, showing plants and roots at different stages of growth. About 160 pages are devoted to Ginseng and more than 50 to Golden Seal—all of interest to growers, diggers and sellers. Some 40 other roots, plants and herbs having medicinal value are shown and briefly described. The raising of not only GINSENG and GOLDEN SEAL (the wild supply of which is nearly gone) but others as well are proving profitable.

This book contains Thirty-five chapters as follows:

I. Plants as a Source of Revenue.
II. List of Plants Having Medicinal Value.
III. Cultivation of Wild Plants.
IV. The Story of Ginseng.
V. Ginseng Habits.
VI. Cultivation.
VII. Shading and Blight.
VIII. Diseases of Ginseng.
IX. Marketing and Prices.
X. Letters from Growers.
XI. General Information.
XII. Medicinal Qualities.
XIII. Ginseng in China.
XIV. Ginseng, Government Description, Etc.
XV. Michigan Mint Farm.
XVI. Miscellaneous Information.
XVII. Golden Seal, Cultivation.
XVIII. Golden Seal, History, Etc.
XIX. Growers' Letters.
XX. Golden Seal — Government Description.
XXI. Cohosh—Black and Blue.
XXII. Snakeroot — Canada and Virginia.
XXIII. Pokeweed.
XXIV. Mayapple.
XXV. Seneca Snakeroot.
XXVI. Lady's Slipper.
XXVII. Forest Plants.
XXVIII. Forest Roots.
XXIX. Thicket Plants.
XXX. Swamp Plants.
XXXI. Field Plants.
XXXII. Dry Soil Plants.
XXXIII. Rich Soil Plants.
XXXIV. Medicinal Plants.
XXXV. Medicinal Shrubs.
XXXVI. Additional Medicinal Plants.

Among the Plants described in Chapters XXVII to XXXV and which furnish Root Drugs are: Male Fern; Wild Turnip; Skunk Cabbage; Sweet Flag; Helonias; American Hellebore; Aletris; Bethroot; Wild Yam; Serpentaria (Southern Snakeroot); Yellow Dock; Soapwort; Goldthread; Oregon Grape; Twinleaf; Canada Moonseed; Bloodroot; Hydrangea; Indian Physic; Wild Indigo; Crane's Bill; Stillinga; Wild Sarsaparilla; Water Eryngo; American Angelica; Yellow Jasmine; Pinkroot; American Colombo; Black Indian Hemp; Pleurisy Root; Comfrey; Stoneroot; Culver's Root; Dandelion; Queen-of-the-Meadow; Elecampane; Echinacea; Burdock. *A good photograph of each is shown with the description.* Considerable money can be made collecting and preparing for the market. This book explains.

A. R. Harding Pub. Co.   2878 E. Main St.—Columbus, Ohio 43209

SCIENCE OF TRAPPING

Describes the Fur Bearing Animals, Their Nature, Habits and Distribution, with Practical Methods of Their Capture.

This book contains 245 pages, 5 x 7 inches, with more than 38 illustrations, many of which are full page of the various fur bearing animals, also several pages of tracks.

The author, Mr. E. Kreps, in his introduction says: "In order to be successful, one must know the wild animals as a mother knows her child. He must also know and use the most practical methods of trapping, and it is my object to give in this work, the most successful trapping methods known. These modes of trapping the fur bearing animals have for the most part been learned from actual experience in various parts of the country, but I also give the methods of other successful trappers, knowing them to be as good as my own. I am personally acquainted with some of the most expert trappers in North America, and have also followed the Indians over their trap lines, and in this way have learned many things which to the white man are not generally known."

This book contains twenty-four chapters, as follows:

1. The Trapper's Art.
2. The Skunk.
3. The Mink.
4. The Weasel.
5. The Marten.
6. The Fisher.
7. The Otter.
8. The Beaver.
9. The Muskrat.
10. The Fox.
11. The Wolf.
12. The Bear.
13. The Raccoon.
14. The Badger.
15. The Opossum.
16. The Lynx.
17. The Bay Lynx or Wild Cat.
18. The Cougar.
19. The Wolverine.
20. The Pocket Gopher.
21. The Rabbit.
22. Tracks and Signs.
23. Handling Furs.
24. Steel Traps.

The chapter on TRACKS AND SIGNS contains sixteen pages — eleven of description and five of illustrations.

The author goes into detail, telling where the tracks and signs of the various animals are most apt to be found. This with an accurate drawing of the footprints, makes the chapter on TRACKS AND SIGNS alone worth dollars to the young and inexperienced trapper, while the distribution, nature, habits, etc., will prove interesting to all. This book is rightly named — Science of Trapping.

A. R. HARDING, Pub., 2878 E. Main St., Columbus, O. 43209